Sisters Revealed

Debbie Manserra

Copyright © Debbie Manserra. 2006
Email:debbie@aci.on.ca

All rights reserved. No part of this book may be reproduced or transmitted in any form or by any means, electronic or mechanical, including photocopying, recording or by any information storage and retrieval system, without written permission from the author, except for the inclusion of brief quotations in a review.

ISBN #1-4196-2487-3

First Edition, 2006

In loving memory of my mother, Nicole.

I dedicate this book to my entire family. Thank you for the wonderful moments shared, and memories to last a lifetime.

A special dedication to my husband Gord: Your unwavering love and constant support clearly shines throughout this book. It was an emotionally challenging endeavour for me but your continuous words of encouragement gave me the confidence to release it to the world. I love you.

"I am the family face;
Flesh perishes, I live on,
Projecting trait and trace
Through time to times anon,
And leaping from place to place
Over oblivion."

Thomas Hardy

PROLOGUE
NICOLE

1961 was a year of new beginnings. In January, Kennedy became the 35th President of the United States of America, heralding a brief period of optimism for America and the West. Russian Cosmonaut Yuri Gagarin became the first man to enter space. And the old world order in the figure of Adolf Eichmann was finally put on trial for crimes against humanity, thus helping lay to rest the ghosts of the Second World War and signaling a new era for people all over the world.

It was a time when the concept of the teenager was just beginning to be born. When North American and European youth began to find their voice and usher in the decade that we now, somewhat symbolically, call the 1960s. 1961 however, saw much more than a chronological beginning of this period of youth; it saw the birth of a new way of thinking, a new horizon, and a new way of life.

Nicole was like any teenager but she was also somehow different. She was seventeen years old and mature for her age. She had need to be; her father suffered long periods of hospitalization with multiple sclerosis, and her mother, Rose, was in and out of hospitals for years with recurring intestinal problems. Nicole not only worked full time to help financially support her family, she also had to play "mother" to her six year old sister, Linda, when Rose was in hospital.

Under these sorts of conditions, you learned to grow up fast and yet, perhaps due to the times that she lived in, Nicole was aware that she was little more than a child herself.

Nicole was very popular with the young men in her neighborhood. She was very beautiful with long chestnut-brown curly hair, Elizabeth Taylor eyes, and a figure every woman longed for. Her social maturity only seemed to add to the attraction the young men had for her, and it found her constantly in trouble with Rose.

Nicole would date men quite frequently, which gave Rose worries beyond the ones she was already dealing with. Her husband's terminal illness and her own weakened health prohibited her from being a full time carer to Nicole and Linda. It was difficult to raise children when the shared burden of marriage was ripped apart by a crippling illness that affected the whole family.

Rose spoke candidly to Nicole about sex and the possibility of pregnancy. Nicole always agreed with Rose and assured her that she wouldn't participate in anything that would hurt her. Despite their problems, Nicole and Rose showed an obvious love for each other that transcended the problems they had; sometimes their relationship resembled that of mother and daughter, sometimes that of friends and equals, but there was always a respect between them that reflected on each of their characters.

Nicole loved and respected her mother. She knew of the hardships her mother had endured in her life due to illness. Rose had contracted tuberculosis shortly before Nicole's birth at a time when it was considered a virtual death sentence. After giving birth, she was taken away to a sanitarium from where it was thought no one ever returned. Every night, she would lie awake amid the coughing and moaning of her fellow patients and dream of her beautiful daughter at home. She was determined to beat the disease and be with her daughter again; she was going to live the life that she knew she deserved.

Rose's mother cared for Nicole during that time. Nicole's memories of that period are vague and misty; however, she frequently told the story of her grandmother being so poor that she had to wear the same booties even after her feet had outgrown them, this was possibly the reason for her unusually high insteps.

Two years after entering the hospital, Rose returned home to her bouncing baby daughter. She was one of the lucky ones; most never left at all.

As she grew up, Nicole turned into a beautiful young woman. She began to frequent a local café in Toronto, Ontario. It was an unassuming place, replicated thousands of times across Canada, America, and Europe. It was here that she would meet with friends and talk about a myriad of small and great things that teenagers fill their time with as they sipped coffee, listened to records and enjoyed being young and free. She was also very rarely without a boyfriend at this time.

PROLOGUE – NICOLE

One day however, she caught sight of a young man, around 21 years old, staring at her from across the café. He was somehow different to the run of the mill boys that she was used to being with; the boys she knew were usually brash and forward, sometimes too forward, as they vied for her attention; trying to catch her eye, to get her address, to get a date with her. This boy however, just stared. He didn't approach her. He seemed too scared.

The man that stared at her was of small build and quite short, even shorter than Nicole who was 5'6". Normally, Nicole would not have been attracted to a man of his build, but there was something about his face. The man had the most beautiful green eyes she had ever seen, and they were enhanced by his olive complexion. It was obvious to Nicole that he was of Italian heritage, but he was gone before she could look at him again.

Nicole started visiting the café without her current boyfriend in the hope of seeing the handsome man who had stared at her. Eventually, she saw him again and beckoned him over to her. As soon as he started to talk, she realized that he *was* Italian and asked him how long he had been in Canada. He told her about his family and their arrival in Canada six years ago. They talked for the rest of the night, never once taking their eyes off each other or realizing there was anyone else in the café. Nicole asked him his name and he replied, "Rocky."

After a few weeks, Nicole broke up with her boyfriend to avail herself to this new Italian man named Rocky. They started dating almost immediately and felt a connection instantaneously.

They had been dating for some weeks when Nicole thought it was time that Rocky meet Rose. Rocky and Rose seemed to get along despite their obvious clash of temperaments. Years later, both Rocky and Nicole would laugh to themselves when they remember how scared they had both been as they stepped through the door to meet Rose.

Months went by and Rose began questioning Rocky's character since he never seemed to have Nicole home on time. Some nights, Nicole would be a few hours late and Rose would stay up worried sick. It was both Rocky and Nicole's fault, and they knew they were at wrong, but their love for one another would always find them in trouble. Their relationship had gone beyond the puppy love stage and had started to become physical. They had been dating for a little over a year when in the spring of 1962 the unexpected happened: Nicole found out she was pregnant. She was shocked and didn't have a clue about what she would do. Nicole told Rocky first, and after his initial upsetting reaction, he did the honorable thing and proposed marriage to her, the girl he loved.

They talked it over between them and decided that this was what they both wanted. Together, they began to imagine their wedding; who they would invite, what plans they would need to make, how they would go about it, where they would have it. But there was still one important thing to be done - they still had to tell Rose. One quiet evening, Nicole sat Rose down and told her. Rose cried and kept repeating that she knew this would happen if Nicole kept dating this Italian man. After venting out her frustrations and anger Rose started to list all the reasons why Nicole couldn't keep the baby; children were expensive, how was Rocky going to support them both? How were they going to cope without a house? Where would they stay? How would they manage? Have they told Rocky's parents? What would the town think?

Rose reminded Nicole of their family situation; her father was still in hospital and Nicole was still needed desperately to look after Linda. Rose was either in hospital with her own condition or visiting her husband; how would they manage with another mouth to feed? How could they cope with another child around the house?

The answer was obvious, Rose thought; Nicole could not keep the baby, and the next day Nicole refused Rocky's hand in marriage.

Nicole worked throughout most of the early stages of her pregnancy and stopped going to see her father. She was from a good Catholic family and this only made the situation more complicated. The last thing Nicole needed, said Rose, was for the community to stare and single her out. Therefore, not even Nicole's father knew the truth. Once she began to show, she hid in the house, venturing out only occasionally. She was kept a prisoner within the confines of her home - even Rocky could not see her - until it was time to give birth.

Nicole gave birth to a beautiful, healthy baby girl on the 3rd of January, 1963, but she did not even get to hold her newborn child before it was carried out of the delivery room and sent away for adoption. Rose was with Nicole during the delivery and she had a good look at the baby. Rose held back her tears as they carried this beautiful baby girl away; she thought the baby looked a lot like Nicole when she had been born. Nicole had to give her baby girl a name for the birth certificate and she named her, Rose Lisa. This was such a heartbreaking time for Nicole and she didn't even have the man she loved, the man who helped create this baby, by her side.

For the briefest of moments, three generations of women had existed in the one room - grandmother, mother, and daughter. It would be the last time for many years, or perhaps, for all they knew, forever. The story was just beginning and the characters that made it still had a long way to go. As Rose Lisa was taken from them, Rose and Nicole felt a hole open up in their lives that would be hard to fill. The first child is a special one; it remains with you for always and never completely lets go. When they took her away, they also took away a part of Rose and Nicole; a part they would never quite forget. After the birth, life went on as usual for Nicole and Rocky. Nicole started working immediately and began visiting her sick father in the hospital again. Rocky's family was never told about the pregnancy; they were unaware that they had a grandchild, a girl, somewhere out there. Rocky, however, had changed; something in him had grown a little darker, a little quieter. He had a baby girl out there somewhere waiting for a family to adopt her. The only people that knew about the pregnancy and adoption were Rose, Nicole, Rocky and Linda, now seven years old.

Nicole and Rocky continued dating but the rules were stricter now. Nicole's curfew was shortened and the frequency of visits, lessened. Nothing however, could keep these two young lovers apart. Every free moment they had, they would find themselves in each other's arms. Nicole started breaking her curfew, and Rose began worrying again. Rose was so upset with Rocky one night that when he rang the doorbell to pick up Nicole, she answered the door and gave him a piece of her mind. She accused him of not loving her daughter and of deliberately ignoring the curfews. She argued that if he respected Nicole, he would want the best for her and leave. Besides, she added, Rocky was too short for her!

Rocky knew he deserved these harsh words but he also knew that if Rose had not denied her daughter marriage, they would have become husband and wife and be raising a daughter of their own. However, he did not hold this against Rose. Rocky knew the hardships her family were dealing with and these hardships didn't seem to be diminishing. But nothing was going to keep these lovers apart.

A year passed quietly with Nicole enjoying her work and appreciating the independence it gave her. She felt as if she was growing into a more beautiful and self-confident young woman everyday. Rose told her many times that there was a whole world waiting to be discovered, that her future lay in front her, and that Rocky need not be a part of it.

Rocky and Nicole still saw each other, however, and their relationship was as passionate as ever. A little over twelve months after the adoption of Rose Lisa, Nicole fell pregnant again with their second child. Once again, Rocky proposed marriage and once again, Nicole refused.

Again, they kept the pregnancy a secret from Rocky's family and history began to repeat itself. Nicole gave birth to a beautiful baby girl on the 11th of September, 1964. This time, Nicole reached out, took her baby and for a brief moment held her in her arms before she was taken away to the adoption center. She named this baby, Lisa Marie.

The next few months were extremely difficult for these two young lovers. Rocky and␣Nicole spoke about the babies sometimes, but it hurt too much to discuss them often. They had given away a piece of their love, a creation they had made together, not once but twice. They only hoped that good families would adopt their daughters and that they would be safe and loved like they so deserved to be.

When they would sit and talk about their children, they wondered where they were and what they looked like; absence did not lessen the love they felt for their family. There was not a day that went past when they did not think of what was missing in their lives, but they decided that whatever happened, they wanted to be together. They still had happiness to find in each other's arms.

Three months after the second birth, Nicole became pregnant again. They could not believe how this could happen so soon after Lisa Marie. When Nicole told Rocky, he announced that he would not stand for another baby to be adopted. He told Nicole that they would marry and raise this child together. Nicole wanted this so much, as much as she did the first and second time, but knew it would be a challenge convincing her mother.

This time Rose did not stand in their way. Of course, she wasn't happy with the news of a third pregnancy since her family's situation had not changed, but she just couldn't bear to see the sadness in her daughter's face for a third time. Nicole and Rocky were so happy; they were finally going to be a family. This upcoming marriage and the birth of their third baby was somewhat easing the pain of the past couple of years. They would be raising this child together as husband and wife.

PROLOGUE – NICOLE

They told Rocky's family for the first time; his family was disappointed and a little shocked that Nicole was pregnant, but they were delighted when Rocky told them that he was going to marry her and raise a family in a manner they would approve of.

Nicole and Rocky were married on the 3rd of April, 1965. It was a very small ceremony with immediate family only, but to Nicole and Rocky, it was the happiest day of their lives. Their third baby was born on the 10th of August, 1965 and again they had a little baby girl. To the rest of the world, including Rocky's family and Nicole's father, this baby girl would be their first child. They named her Tina Marie.

For the first time, they felt that they were the family they had always wanted to be. Tina would cry all night and sleep all day, but it didn't matter, they had never been happier. They lived with Rose and Linda shortly after the birth of Tina and this worked out well. Nicole could continue working while helping out her family and Rose looked after Tina as much as she could.

Just after Tina's first birthday, Nicole found out that she was pregnant again. She and Rocky were thrilled with the news. This child was planned for and conceived during their marriage. This time everything felt right and nothing could go wrong; this time things would be in place, and they would no longer have to worry about what people thought or how their news would be taken.

While Nicole was carrying her fourth child, her father passed away. He had been terribly ill for many years but, as always, the death of a parent is a difficult thing to come to terms with. The funeral was long and exhausting for Nicole. She could see that her mother was grieving but could also see the relief in her mother's eyes. He had suffered with Multiple Sclerosis for almost ten years, and he had spent the better part of the last four years in the hospital. His illness had taken the life out of Rose. Finally, Rose could look after herself and her youngest daughter properly. This also meant that at last, Nicole was free to be mother to her own children and no one else.

On the 4th of October, 1967, Nicole and Rocky were blessed with another baby girl. They named her Deborah Ann. It is strange how the birth of another child never fills the gap left by an adoption or a death, but it helps take some of the pain away by deflecting and directing ones attention and thoughts elsewhere. Nicole was kept busy with changing diapers, changing beds, feeding, and finding clothes; these things somehow lessened and made bearable the original ache of losing a child.

Less than two years after the birth of Deborah came the arrival of their first son on the 14th of March, 1969. They named him Leonard Andrew, Lenny for short. Three years after Lenny came the birth of their second son, Rocky Christopher, on the 7th of May, 1972. They were now a family of four; two girls and two boys and they were as complete as any family could ever be. Nicole had gone through six pregnancies and six births.

1961 was a time of upheaval for the world. It began with the election of John F. Kennedy, an act of almost universal optimism, and ended with the first helicopters flying into Vietnam in December. It was easy to see that the world was changing and that it would never be the same again. This was true also for Nicole, who would never again be the teenager that she once was. However, it is perhaps neither happy nor easy times that change us most, but sadness and difficulty; it is in those times that we test who we really are and experience our true selves.

Nicole and Rocky had weathered the storms of their early marriage and become closer; it was as if the negativity and criticism of their own families had pushed them into becoming a unit of one at first, and later, a unit of six. In their hearts, however, they held onto their secret; it was best kept with them. Like many young couples at this time, they did whatever they had to do on their own with very little help or guidance. Years later, they still carried the scars and the smiles of that with them.

1.
INTRODUCING ME, DEBBIE

I consider myself an ordinary person with an ordinary life. My family was ordinary too, consisting of one older sister, two younger brothers, parents and two sets of grandparents. At least, my life was what I considered to be ordinary until the age of 25 when I found out I had two other siblings; two sisters who were given away for adoption at birth; two sisters who were conceived by my parents.

My earliest memory is of being at my Aunt Rhoda and Uncle Charlie's house on the Danforth in Toronto. Uncle Charlie would call me "Démama" as he held out his arms for me to jump into. I would sit on his lap while taking in the scent of his pipe; it smelled so sweet. Afterwards, we would walk to the shops in town to buy candy. I loved being in their home because it was so full of laughter and love.

It wasn't until years later that I found out the meaning of my nickname; it meant, "little mother" - apparently, I had displayed traits of a mother from a very young age. Aunt Rhoda and Uncle Charlie were in fact my great aunt and uncle. Uncle Charlie and my grandmother, Mèmere Rose, were brother and sister; but growing up I only knew them as my favorite aunt and uncle.

Memère Rose cared for my sister Tina during the week, while my parents worked to make ends meet. Tina lived to her own schedule that consisted of sleeping all day and being most alert during the night. When my brother Lenny was born, we lived in the basement of Memère Rose's cute bungalow on Malamute Street in Agincourt, Ontario. Tina and I shared a small bedroom and slept in bunk beds. When Lenny's crib arrived, our small bedroom became overcrowded, but as squashed as we were in our tiny room, we managed. He was a pretty good baby and always made our sleeping arrangements bearable.

Many nights I would awake with either my legs or ears aching. My Mom took care of me by putting warm oil on a cotton ball and placing them in my ears. I'm not completely certain if this was a useful remedy but for some reason it eased the pain. More than likely it was my Mom's arms around me, holding and rocking me until I fell asleep that soothed the pain away. Dad took care of my aching legs by rubbing them and telling me it was just growing pains. He said that when I grew up, I would have good strong legs that could carry me for miles.

I started school when I was only 4 years old because my birthday fell in October. I remember crying on the first day and feeling intimidated and afraid. I kept my own company and prayed for the day to be over. It was such a relief when I saw Tina and Memère Rose waiting for me at the school gates, ready to walk me home. Our public school, Lynngate, was only a short distance away from our house but in the winter months, it seemed like miles away.

There was a small hill on the school property and during winter, Mom would bundle us up and pull us by sleigh. We enjoyed the speed as we slid down the hill. When we returned home, we would build an igloo out of snow in the backyard to protect us from the winds.

Like most kids, I suppose, our favorite time of year was Christmas. It would begin with dinner with Memère Rose and Leandre where the food was so plentiful we would leave the table with bellies as full as a stuffed turkey. After dinner, we gathered around Memère Rose's Christmas tree and opened our presents while Christmas tunes - I mostly recall Englebert Humperdink and Kenny Rogers - played in the background. We had most fun singing along to "Deck the Halls" but my favorite Christmas carol was "What Child Is This?"

On Christmas Day, we always visited our father's parents, whom we called Memère and Pèpere, even though they were Italian and should have been called Nona and Nono. For some reason, Mom's French heritage won out. Once again, we ate too much and opened more presents from our grandparents and our father's sister, Aunt Tina.

We would complete the holiday festivities at Uncle Mario's house on New Year's Day. After more delicious food and presents, it was over all too soon. It seemed magical while it lasted.

I lost my beautiful baby teeth at a very young age only to be burdened with gigantic crooked new ones. I never realized how bad they were until I was at a wading pool with Tina and Lenny one day. I enjoyed swimming and especially holding my breath under water. While under water, I bumped into some boy and when I came up, he yelled and called me "fat tooth." Tina and Lenny laughed but from that moment onwards, I became very self-conscious of my teeth. My parents couldn't afford braces and the school dental nurse always sent me home with a report indicating that I required them. So, I decided to take matters into my own hands by secretly wearing an elastic band around my upper teeth at night in hopes of straightening them.

I had a slight speech impediment at this time and couldn't pronounce the letter, r. This caused me huge amounts of embarrassment at school because I was taken out of class for speech therapy once a week. The therapist would make me repeat "Rocky the rabbit ran across the street," and it was nearly impossible to pronounce one word correctly. I eventually did it, but it took going to summer school for speech therapy for a couple of years in a row. After that time, I was no longer referred to as Elmer Fudd!

Eventually Tina and I moved out of the cramped tiny bedroom that we shared with Lenny to a spare room upstairs beside Memère Rose and Leandre. Lenny and Rocky now occupied the bunk beds that were once mine and Tina's. We made the most of what we had on Malamute Street; great friends, great family and good health. Our stay with my grandparents ended in the summer of 1978. It was good timing since Tina and I were both starting new schools; I was starting junior high and Tina, high school.

My family moved out of Memère Rose's house when I was eleven. We moved into a large, three bedroom condominium in Scarborough, Ontario. Naturally, it felt scary at first since we would have to make new friends. However, we liked our new digs; mostly, the indoor pool and sauna. It made up for the lack of a backyard. At that time, Dad also started his own billiard hall business, and we helped him out during our summer break. It was enormous with over 25 snooker tables; he even hosted the Canadian Snooker Championships there.

I was a typical teenager at this time; going out with boys, catching their eye, and them catching mine. The teenage years are the ones we remember most, perhaps, because these are the ones that form who we are to be as adults. The child can be changed easily by experience but the mistakes and the decisions we make during the teenage years stick with us forever, like a layer of skin that protects us.

This is also a time of contradiction and conflict; on the one hand, you are desperate to assert yourself and on the other, you are eager to fit in. I argued with Dad over the usual things that pass between father and daughter such as make-up, clothes, and staying out late. However, he mostly did not approve of my boyfriends since they were always older and more experienced than I was. Eventually, he gave me an ultimatum and I chose to leave. I had just finished high school and was working for Dad full time at his new business; a sports and social club. It meant that I had to find a new job as well and put my anticipated education on hold.

I did find a new job. I was just turning eighteen when I started work as a receptionist at a local company. It didn't pay a lot of money, but I enjoyed the work and within two years I doubled my salary. The best part was meeting and becoming good friends with a wonderful man, Gord, sixteen years my senior. He initially seemed a little forward and obnoxious, but these were qualities which oddly enough became intriguing. We started dating when I turned nineteen, and two years later in 1988, we were married. I got married at the young age of twenty-one, following in my Mom's and sister's footsteps.

The glue that holds marriages together is hardship. I was often told that the more you love someone, the easier it is to cope when things go wrong; it is as if the two of you somehow add up to more than you could ever possibly be individually. Our first experience of this came early in the morning.

At 5:30 a.m. on the 5th of May, 1991, a loud banging at our apartment door awakened us. I stayed in bed while Gord answered it. I didn't hear much noise, just sporadic low voices and I thought it was a neighbor of ours. But something suddenly felt terribly wrong, so I got out of bed and went into the living room. As soon as I saw who was sitting with Gord, it all became very clear to me. Gord was awfully pale and his brother was silent. I felt paralyzed but managed to hold Gord. I couldn't speak, but what words could I have possibly said to ease the painful news he had just heard. His mother had just passed away a few hours before, after a brief battle with cancer.

The funeral took place a few days later. My heart ached for Gord and his family. She was only fifty-eight and taken away from us so suddenly. Life just didn't seem fair and we basically drifted for a while. Everything seemed like a dream that we just blindly walked through from one moment to the next. We all think we might live forever, and we certainly never expect our parents to die so suddenly and so soon. But it is these things that strengthen us and drive us closer. Death seems to bring out a side to a person that truly exposes their inner self, including a softness, which many men would be reluctant to expose.

Like every life experience, we pulled through it. Gord felt very fortunate to have had such a close relationship with his mother. I also felt close to her, even in the short amount of time I was blessed with knowing her. She was a wonderful lady who left me with fond memories.

Gord and I were determined to get closer to our respective families, and to never let them forget that we were there for them or that we loved them. About a year after the death of his mother, Gord received a phone call that was to turn our lives upside down, once again.

We were sitting leisurely in our swivel rockers and chatting before bedtime. It was about 10:30 p.m. when the phone rang. Gord answered and all I could hear was, "Yes, this is Gord, John's son. You can talk to me." Then I heard, "How bad is he? What do you want to operate on?" At this point, my eyes filled with tears, and my heart felt like it was in my throat. Gord told the doctor that he would be there as soon as possible and gave him permission over the phone to go ahead and operate.

When Gord put the phone down, he looked at me and said that his father had been in a very serious car accident. He was in a critical condition at Kingston Hospital, which was approximately a three-hour car ride from our home.

I remember thinking to myself that this couldn't be happening. Gord couldn't lose his father after losing his mother just a year ago. Gord was almost on his way out the door when I told him that I wanted to come along. He assumed that I wouldn't because I had just started a new job that week. I didn't give it a second thought. I just knew that I wanted to be there for my husband and his father.

We arrived at the hospital in just under two hours. Gord's father was barely recognizable in his swollen body. I felt sick to my stomach. Gord felt relieved when he saw his father moving and fighting to get up. Gord said that he knew his father would live, since every part of his father's body seemed to be functioning. Unfortunately, the doctor wasn't as optimistic; Gord's father's vitals were very weak and an infection had taken over his body.

We left the room and went to the hospital chapel to say a few prayers. I guess our prayers were answered because his vitals were much improved the next day. Gord's father sustained injuries that would have killed most people: ten broken ribs, one punctured lung, two compound fractured arms, a broken neck, and a serious eye laceration. Not to mention the fact that he was sixty-four years old.

Three weeks after being admitted, Gord's father left the hospital a whole lot thinner and with a halo-vest around his neck. But he was alive and mostly well. He was also very determined to regain his strength and to get on with life. He never did remember what caused him to drive off the highway and hit a tree; not that it mattered since it was obvious that it wasn't his time to leave this world.

Gord's family was strong, and I was determined to stand by him and help him as much as I could. We needed a new start, something that would signal our intent for the future and our life together. We decided to move and found the perfect place in Aurora, Ontario.

It was on the 31st of July, 1992, that we spent our first night together in the big, brand new house. Our house wasn't that large, but it seemed so in comparison to the 650 square foot, one-bedroom apartment that Gord and I had been living in. My family had never owned their own house and from the age of eleven, I had lived in apartments. I couldn't wait for Mom to see it; I wanted her to see how proud I was at having finally taken a huge step towards being a mature, responsible adult.

Mom wasn't feeling well but I convinced her to spend a weekend with us in the next couple of weeks. Mom had never driven a car so I picked her up on a Friday evening. When we pulled up to the driveway, she blurted out, "*This* is your house?" As we entered, I could see tears fill her eyes. She was overjoyed and very proud of us. I gave her the grand tour and she loved every room. All of a sudden, I felt saddened and almost embarrassed that I was showing off my home. I'm sure Mom wished she could have been as fortunate as I was when she was twenty-four.

We spent a wonderful evening eating, laughing, and talking together. Mom mentioned that she wasn't eating as well as usual, and that her sleeping patterns had changed. I was a little concerned, but Mom had experienced these problems in the past and they were usually to do with her diet. She slept in until 9 a.m. the next morning and was shocked when she realized the time. She never slept in that late; she always woke up at 6 a.m., even on the weekends.

We shopped all day, and I showed her my new hometown of Aurora. Dad showed up for dinner and the four of us spent a quiet evening together. My parents were quite impressed with my cooking, and I gave them the credit for that. I was part French and part Italian so my genes contributed to my natural ability to cook well. After dinner, my parents left together.

As I watched them walk down the driveway, I felt as if my life was making sense at last; I had moved into the house of my dreams with the man of dreams. I was so pleased to be able to share my dream with my parents who now saw me as a woman instead of a little girl.

Two weeks later, I received a call from Mom; the doctor told her that she needed her gall bladder removed. She was nervous but relieved to know that there was an explanation for her recent stomach problems, and she would feel better soon. She was scheduled to be operated upon in the later part of August; the doctor didn't want to delay the surgery due to concerns about her age.

A couple of days before the surgery, Mom called me at home and sounded extremely emotional. The doctor had informed her that her liver was enlarged and that the x-ray had shown a small tumor. It took all my energy and strength not to cry over the phone, but I felt I had to be strong for her. I told her not to worry since it was probably nothing and that the surgery would be over before she knew it. My words seemed to calm her a little, but I had never known my Mom to be scared; it was strange and frightening to hear it in the voice of a woman who was usually so self-assured and brave. She told me she loved me - something she rarely verbalized - and I told her that I loved her as well.

I was overcome as I put down the phone; I couldn't hold back my emotions any longer, the mere thought of my Mom having cancer so soon after the loss of Gord's mother was too much to bear. Gord held me in his arms and reassured me that everything would be all right. Through my tears, I told him that if Mom died I would go crazy and would not be able to handle it.

I spoke with my sister Tina the next day, and we both agreed to visit Mom at the hospital on Monday. We planned to meet at Aunt Linda's house before going to the hospital. When we arrived at Aunt Linda's house, our grandmother, Memère Rose, was there as well. Memère Rose lived two hours away but had spent the weekend with Aunt Linda. I asked Aunt Linda and Memère Rose how Mom was doing since they had visited the hospital earlier that morning. They said she was fine and that I could ask her myself soon. I felt uneasy with the way they looked and how evasive they were, but I didn't press them with questions since Tina and I would soon be at the hospital.

It was about noon when Tina and I arrived at the hospital. We hurried to Mom's room. Mother was sharing a room with another patient who had her daughter visiting her when we arrived. Mom was sitting up in her bed, looking pretty in her light blue nightdress with her make-up applied on as beautifully as it always was. She certainly didn't look like a woman who had just had major surgery.

Tina and I kissed her and asked how she was feeling. She said she felt fine but had something to tell us. She didn't change the tone of her voice or her poise as she said the most feared words anyone could ever imagine hearing from a parent: "I have cancer." She explained that they opened her up to operate but immediately stopped the procedure. The doctor told her that she was full of cancerous growth primarily in the liver. Unfortunately, there was no treatment available at this late stage - not chemotherapy or radiation or operation - there was absolutely nothing to help her. She then told us in a positive, cheerful manner that they had given her up to six months to live.

Mom was not even crying when she spoke these horrible words. Tina and I started bawling like babies, and Mom tried to comfort us. I kept saying to myself that this must be a bad dream that I hoped to wake up from. I told Mom that I didn't believe that there was no cure for her and that we would figure something out, and that she would be fine. I didn't really know what I was saying, but there was no way I would accept this defeat. No way on earth would I let my Mom die without doing my best to help her stay alive. Mom was holding us and being such a brave and courageous woman. Tina and I wanted to hold Mom and let her know everything would be sorted out; however, as so often happened throughout our lives, she was the one doing the consoling.

I was twenty-four and Tina twenty-seven, but I suddenly thought of my younger brothers; how were they going to react to this earth shattering news? How could they cope? Lenny was twenty-three and Rocky was only twenty. They both still lived at home. About an hour after Tina and I had been informed of Mom's illness, Lenny came into the room to visit with her. He could instantly tell that something was wrong because Tina and I both had swollen eyes. With Lenny, Mom once again bravely spoke of her condition. Lenny just cried and held her, too stunned to do anything else.

The patient in the bed next to Mom's became emotional after overhearing Mom's news, even her daughter was holding back tears. They just looked at us, and I could see how sad they felt for us. I felt bad that they had to witness our emotional outbursts so I drew close the curtains that separated Mom's bed from the other patient's, to try to alleviate some of the grief.

INTRODUCING ME, DEBBIE

I left Mom's hospital room and went outside for some air. I felt like I was drowning, and my stomach was aching. I knew that I had to make a few calls; I couldn't hold it off any longer. The first call was to my parents' home in hope of reaching my youngest brother, Rocky. He didn't answer, so I proceeded to call Dad at work. Mom had urged me not to say anything to him, because she wanted tell him tomorrow, when she was home. But my gut instinct told me to call. Dad answered the phone, and I told him to get over to the hospital immediately. He asked me what was wrong. I just told him to get here.

When I returned to Mom's hospital room, Rocky had just arrived. When he was told the devastating news, his face looked blank and unemotional. He appeared to be in complete denial, and he didn't want to hear anymore. We just let Rocky be, as he sat around not saying a word. I guess everybody handles grief in different ways.

About half an hour later, Dad showed up; his eyes filled with tears even before he was told what was wrong. Then, when Mom told him the news, he wept on her lap. Mom finally broke down and we were all so distraught. My parents weren't what I considered close, even after their twenty-seven years of marriage, but this was an extremely emotional time. This devastating news brought them closer than they had been for many years.

I could barely breathe anymore so Tina and I went for a walk. She had to call her husband, and I wanted to call Gord. My fingers were trembling as I dialed Gord's number. He answered and said cheerfully, "There you are. I've been trying to call you. How's your Mom?" My voice cracked as I managed to say, "She has liver cancer and she's going to die within six months." There were a few moments of silence on the other end of the line before Gord started saying that he would call his father and somehow find a liver for Mom. I had pondered that thought, but we both knew in our hearts that there was no cure for liver cancer at a late stage. I cried on the phone. Gord asked if I was okay to drive and if not, he would come and get me. I told him that I'd be all right to drive and would be leaving shortly.

We hugged Mom goodnight and told her that we'd see her the next day, at her home. She said she wasn't up to a welcome home party but that we could drop by.

Once I was driving home by myself, I broke down completely. I cried so hard that I had a hard time seeing the road. I knew I had to stop because, I couldn't drive safely. I pulled over to the side of the road and wept bitterly. I felt like the world was about to end; perhaps, it already had.

When I finally reached home, Gord hugged and held me tightly as I sobbed in his arms. All I could say was, "Why *my* Mom?" She was only forty-eight, and she had never harmed a soul.

The next day Gord and I visited Mom at her home. I noticed that she didn't have the energy she normally had; in fact, she seemed worse than the previous day at the hospital. We didn't stay long because she needed to rest.

The following day, both Dad and I contacted the doctor to get his opinion. He gave us the same information that Mom had given us, except to say that Mom probably wouldn't make it to Christmas.

There was absolutely nothing any of us could do to help her; the whole family had never felt so helpless.

I wanted to spend as much time with Mom as possible, but I could only visit her every other evening; I had a full time job and lived a forty-five minute drive away. Memère Rose had planned to stay with Mom until the time came for Mom to be admitted to the hospital. Mom was grateful to have Memère Rose take care of her as she had when she was a little girl. I guess it was the second week in September when Mom became jaundiced. My heart broke to see her this way but luckily, she wasn't in pain.

Mom spoke to me candidly about her death and described the outfit she wanted to wear when in her casket. She asked me to stay in touch with Dad and ensure that my brothers would be okay, since they were single and still living at home. She also wanted me to maintain a relationship with my Italian grandparents.

I guess Mom felt that I was, emotionally, the strongest one in the family. I was trying my best to be strong for her and in my will to carry out her wishes. These wishes were actually pretty silly since I didn't need her to tell me; I loved these people and hopefully I would have a relationship with them forever. I have always kept in touch with my family and never forgot things like birthdays; I was often told that I was like my Mom in that respect.

As soon as I left Mom's room, I broke down. But I didn't want her to see my pain as I knew it would upset her.

Mom seemed to get worse as the days went by. The morphine she was taking was starting to play with her mind. She was still quite coherent, but she would get confused occasionally. She would say things I didn't understand or remember things that never happened or seem to be dreaming while still awake.

On my 25th birthday, Gord bought me a birthday cake, and we took it over to my parents' house; my brothers and Memère Rose were also there. Mom was in bed and apparently having a rough day. I kept holding back tears at the thought that this would be my last birthday with her. It seemed unreal, like I was living in the twilight zone or having a horrible nightmare. Mom was too weak to get out of bed and was somewhat confused, so we proceeded to have a light lunch while she rested.

When it was time to cut the cake, everyone - except the most important woman in my life, my Mom - had gathered around, singing Happy Birthday. They were halfway through the song when Mom came running out suddenly to join in the singing. She used the word anniversary instead of birthday, but that didn't matter one bit to me. I was simply overjoyed that she had somehow managed to find the strength to join in; she had made my last birthday with her a special one. My heart filled with so much love for her that I had to hold back my tears while trying to blow out the candles. I didn't bother to make a wish, since I knew that the only wish I wanted, would not come true.

Mom presented me with a birthday card; she had signed, in slanted writing, "To Debbie, love Nicole." I had a difficult time reading it through my tearful, blurred vision.

Aunt Linda had obviously bought the card on Mom's behalf and had even written "Mom" in brackets, after "Nicole" But that did not matter to me; the important thing was the effort Mother had made by signing a card.

I would have these memories with me forever, for all my birthdays to follow. I will not only remember the sadness in my heart but also remember the strength of one incredible lady.

Shortly after my birthday, Mom took a turn for the worst and was hospitalized. I received a call at work from Gord. He said he was on his way to pick me up because the doctor had called Dad and told him that he better get to the hospital. We were all at the hospital expecting it to be Mom's last day. But Mom came to and casually said, "I'm not going yet, but thanks for visiting!" I thanked God that it was a false alarm and she was still with us.

However, Mom was weak, so she was placed into palliative care and monitored constantly. We all knew that her being surrounded by other dying patients was the worst part for her. She would say to us, "I wonder when it's my turn," and we would try to reassure and comfort her as best we could.

Memère Rose and Aunt Linda would take turns to see her during the day. Tina and my brothers would spend late afternoons and evenings with her. Dad would visit during the day and often late into the night; sometimes, he would spend the night in a cot beside her bed.

Sometimes, I would watch her facial expressions as she slept; she often wore a smile when asleep, dreaming. I wanted to spend as much time with her as possible, and be a good daughter during the good and bad days. I would hold her hand and try to comfort the woman who had raised me; she had always made me feel so safe and loved. It was now my turn to make her feel safe and loved.

She hadn't liked Gord when we had first started dating because of his age. But one day, as I sat by her, she told me that I had a very good man, and that I should hold onto him. She also told me how much she loved me and what a thoughtful daughter I was. This meant so much to me; not because I didn't already know it, but because it felt good just to hear her say it.

I never knew what to expect when I entered Mom's palliative care room: a Mom with a big smile, and face painted beautifully or a jaundiced looking woman who barely recognized me and spoke very little, if at all. All my memories of her held vivid sounds of her laugh; high pitched and contagious. My friends had always commented on how much they loved her laugh.

I was home alone one evening when the telephone rang. I had hated to hear the phone ring ever since the death of Gord's mother and the near death of his father. Its harsh ring always reminded me of bad news and of feeling as if the world was getting a little darker, or coming to an end. I walked over to the telephone and picked up the receiver, gingerly.

It was Aunt Linda. I recognized her voice immediately and, all of a sudden, a thousand thoughts rushed into my head. I did not want to hear what she had to say, I just wanted to put the phone down and ignore whatever bad news there was.

We began to talk about Mom and about how she had been. We chatted about our memories and the times she and Mom had shared; the early days of Mom's marriage, and of Dad courting her. Aunt Linda talked easily of those years even though she was young at the time. She also talked about the death of her father, and the house she and Mom shared with Memère Rose. It felt good to be talking like this; talking of Mom's past as if it was the narrative of a book or the plot of a movie somehow made her seem more special.

Then, she mentioned something that would change my life forever; a secret so strange and unthinkable that, for a moment, I let her words wash over me.

She said, "You have two other sisters out there somewhere. Your Mom gave them away for adoption before Tina was born."

I was stunned and asked her to repeat it, which she did. I could feel myself shake as if the ground was moving underneath my feet. This could not be true; it could not be real. My Mom - whom I knew so well, who had been there for me all my life and who now, even though so weak, was still unafraid - could not have done such a thing and kept it hidden for all these years.

The questions just flew from my mouth as I asked, "When did this happen? Is Dad the father? Where did they go? Did they get adopted out together?" I inundated her with questions because naturally, there was a certain amount of doubt in my mind of whether what she told me was in fact true.

Aunt Linda told me that Mom had only been seventeen at the time of her first pregnancy. She said that Mom hid in the basement until she had the baby and had given it away at birth. After a year, the same scenario was repeated; the pregnancy, the hiding away, the baby girl and the adoption. She told me that no one else saw Mom pregnant and that only she, Dad and Memère Rose knew of Mom's pregnancy.

I was utterly overwhelmed by this information, and I just wanted to get off the phone. I had so many other questions but at that point, I just had one burning question for Aunt Linda, "Why are you telling me all this now?"

Aunt Linda said that when she visited Mom - who was under morphine medication -recently, she had mentioned the two girls she had given away all those years ago. Aunt Linda and Mom have never discussed the adoptions before. Aunt Linda was afraid that Mom might say something to the family and we would think that she was going crazy. Aunt Linda wanted to tell one of us the truth just in case Mom said anything about the adoptions; she was afraid that we might think Mom was going crazy if she mentioned it herself.

I thought of my Mom in her hospital bed, too tired to move for a great deal of time yet still looking beautiful in a way that only my Mom could. I couldn't believe that she would do anything to hurt anyone. She must have had her reasons but I couldn't think what they were. Suddenly, I felt as if the family I knew wasn't there anymore; I still had the same family I've always had, but somehow there was a part, an important part missing. When you are the second oldest child in a family, you feel as though you know your place; you feel as though the world you live in is how it should be. When you realize you have two more siblings, you begin to question that place and that world.

After I hung up the phone, I sat frozen in my swivel rocker. I could not move a muscle. I couldn't even cry. I just sat there numb to the outside world. How could it be true?

I told Gord the news and he sat beside me, looking pretty pale himself. He began asking me questions that were not dissimilar to the ones I had asked Aunt Linda; except he added a few questions that would provide factual answers. "What years were the girls adopted out? What was your Mom's maiden name? What city did she give them away in?" It dawned on me that Gord was trying to gather information so that he could verify the accuracy of what I had just found out. I had no idea how he would accomplish this task, but I knew if anyone could it, it would be my husband and his tenacity.

That night I barely slept a wink. I contemplated calling Tina but decided to wait until I knew a few more facts. I couldn't believe what I had just been told. How on earth could I have just gained two sisters and never known about them before? What if I had bumped into one or both of them in the past; I would never have known. Suddenly, the Mom I had known for so long seemed like a stranger to me.

2.
REVELATIONS

The next morning, I felt as though the world had changed. Suddenly, the things that I had taken for granted were different somehow; the familiar things had altered. I awoke and opened up the shutters to a street that looked the same but felt different. I did not know if I would ever get back to where I was the day before yesterday. I had to hurry to get to work on time, I had overslept which was something I very rarely did; that itself was testament to how I was feeling. Gord said that he was going to look into the situation and call me if he found anything.

My car did not want to start. The route was more crowded than usual, and it was bitterly cold even though it was only October. I felt as if I had slipped into a parallel universe that was the same but irretrievably foreign; the people I knew, those who were closest to me, had kept from me something that would change my whole life.

I had been at work for about an hour when Gord called to tell me that he was speaking with the Catholic Children's Aid Society. He had told the councilor on the other end that he required information to be confirmed for his wife. He had informed the councilor of the circumstances surrounding Mom's illness, and the urgency in knowing as many facts as they were willing to confirm.

They verbally confirmed to Gord that two adoptions had occurred in the early 1960s under my Mom's maiden name. However, in order to obtain any further information I would have to write a letter to the society, requesting non-identifying information regarding my adopted siblings.

So it was true! I sat at my desk and let the phone fall. Somewhere, God knows where, I had two sisters who didn't even know I existed. I said goodbye to Gord, put the phone back on the hook and sat for a while silently staring at the desk, unable to think or comprehend the enormity of what I had just been told. My emotions at this time were more of shock than anger or bitterness. I did not feel resentment towards my parents, merely shock, since what I had known to be my life and my family had suddenly shifted and become noticeably different. All I knew was that I had to share this information with Tina. She had a right to know, and I hoped that we could emotionally support each other.

Perhaps not thinking rationally, I called Tina at work. She answered the phone in a cheerful voice, and I instantly wondered whether I had made the right decision in calling her. I took a deep breath and told her of the conversation I had with Aunt Linda the night before. I also told her that Gord had authenticated the information this morning. The line fell silent. I apologized for calling her at work but she still did not speak.

She broke her silence after a while; the strain in her voice was palpable. She mentioned that she had found a picture of a newborn baby that she did not recognize at my parent's home recently. When she questioned Memère Rose about it, Memère Rose told her that the picture was not of any of us, and that she would talk more about it later. Tina had dismissed the picture; after all, many families have baby pictures of distant relatives and work colleagues' children in their collection of pictures. She thought that this picture was no different; that it was merely one of those things. But it was more than just one of those things; suddenly, the picture made sense. The baby was one of us, one of our family members.

During our conversation, Tina and I used the words "our sisters" and we both felt strange saying them. For so long, we both had only one sister, each other. We didn't speak for too long since we were both at work. I told her we'd talk more that night.

I went to visit Mom after work. When I arrived, the nurses let me know she had not had a very good day but was now sleeping soundly. I walked into the room quietly, and the lady across from my Mom's bed waved to me before putting a finger across her mouth, signaling me to be quiet. I did not say a word; I just pulled up a chair and sat next to Mom's bed. The only sounds I could hear were the distant hums of a busy hospital, but even that couldn't break this moment or dare intrude on its sacredness.

I just looked at her silently, full of questioning thoughts: "Mom, why didn't you ever tell us about our sisters? Why did you feel you had to keep it a secret? Why do I feel like I don't know you now?" I held her hand and cried quietly. She looked so peaceful that it took all my strength not to wake her and ask her these questions aloud. As I watched her sleep, I realized that there had to be good reasons why she and Dad had kept this information from us for all these years, and to discuss it now would be disrespectful. So, I decided not to burden her with the revelation that I knew her secret. She was dying, and I didn't think it was fair, at least for the moment, to force her to relive what must have been so painful for her.

Outside the hospital, people were coming and going unmindful of what was happening to my family. Children were visiting relatives, patients were coming and going for treatment, doctors were walking briskly past me. Then it hit me: Mom was younger than I when all this happened. She was barely a woman at all and had to bear this largely on her own, for all these years. She must have felt something missing at every birthday and Christmas, and yet, she hid it from the rest of us because she loved us so much.

On my drive home I realized that maybe Mom felt she was dying so early in life because she had given away two babies. Maybe she figured death was her punishment. I'm sure that was the reason for Mom even mentioning the baby girls to Aunt Linda. Maybe it would be a good idea to let Mom know that Tina and I knew the secret and that we were not upset about it. There was no reason for Mom to feel guilty as far as I was concerned. There was a part of me that didn't want Mom to die without her knowing that we had found out her secret and that maybe one day, we would even meet our two sisters.

It suddenly hit home that Mom's words were not borne from the confusion of an ill woman, but a confession of someone desperate to make amends after all these years. Mom had in effect not been talking to Aunt Linda, but to Tina, my brothers and me, and the sisters we did not know we had. She had, perhaps, wanted us to find and bring them into the family after being apart from us for all this time.

I still didn't know what to do, but I decided to keep silent and wait to see how Mom fared. Tina and I both felt it unnecessary to burden any other family members at a time like this. I was glad that we at least had each other to confide in.

Mom had good days, bad days and days where she seemed unaware of the condition she was in. She hadn't walked for about a month and her feet and legs were swollen. I remember visiting her one particular evening, and when I entered her room she looked absolutely beautiful. Her hair was swept up into a messy bun with curls hanging in perfect spirals to the sides of her painted face. Mom was sitting up and when she saw me, she asked where I had been because she missed me. As I hugged her I told her that she looked lovely and that I had missed her as well; I didn't bother to mention that I had sat by her the night before.

Days were flying by and my only mission was to make sure Mom was fine and not in any pain, physically at least. I visited often and had many sleepless nights wondering if that night would be the last night I would speak to the Mom I so dearly loved.

Halloween was a few days away and Gord attempted to make Mom's room festive. However, the ghosts and goblins didn't go over so well with the three other patients who shared her room. Mom thought it was fun and that the decorations were great, but she asked us to take all the scary stuff home since the other patients were frightened. Halloween was always a fun holiday for Mom. She would spend hours filling loot bags with an assortment of candy. When we were children, we all had fabulous costumes. But Halloween was not the only important event on October 31st; it was also the date of Memère's birthday.

I would speak to Mom for the last time on the 31st of October, 1992. It was a Saturday and Memère Rose had spent most of the day with her and was traveling back home to be with her husband that evening after almost two months. She had stayed for a month at Mom's house before she was hospitalized, and another month at Aunt Linda's house after; so it was time for Memère Rose to see her husband and spend a little time back home.

I didn't even get to see Memère Rose to wish her a happy birthday. She had already left when Gord and I arrived. I thought Mom was sleeping when we entered her room, but I was wrong. Mom was in a coma. I didn't know if she could hear me, but I couldn't help myself from weeping. I looked at her face, so jaundiced and still. Her body was covered with huge lumps that could no longer be disguised with a blanket. Mom never spoke a word and just lay sleeping. We didn't stay long since it hurt me far too much to see her so lifeless. I hoped Mom would wake up and that tomorrow would be a much better day for her, but I somehow felt that the end was nearing.

That night we received a phone call from Dad's sister, inviting us for breakfast the next morning. Dad's brother, Tony, had just arrived in Toronto from his hometown in Florida, and he wanted to meet us all for breakfast. I declined the invitation since my mood was extremely saddened at the sight of Mom from that evening.

I awoke the next morning to the sound of my husband telling me that Mom's doctor was on the phone. I stumbled to get to the receiver. The doctor informed me that Mom was in a really bad condition and advised me to get to the hospital right away. It was around 8:30 a.m. when I put the phone down. I got out of bed and ran downstairs. Gord was sitting in the family room and was unsure about what I had just been told; but, it was obvious from his expression that he anticipated the worst. He hugged me and poured me some coffee as I told him that I wasn't sure if I wanted to go to the hospital right away.

Gord and I sat in the kitchen drinking coffee when I noticed that it was a glorious, sunny day. Our kitchen beamed with sunlight, and I don't think I had ever seen a sky more blue. I was on my second cup of coffee when the phone rang again. This time, it was one of the nurses in the Palliative Care Unit calling to tell me that Dad had been with Mom for the last few hours by himself. She thought I should hurry to the hospital. I was somewhat confused since Dad's family were all supposed to be having breakfast together at a restaurant. I figured Dad must have received a call from the doctor similar to the call I'd had earlier.

As I was getting dressed around 10 a.m., the phone rang again and this time, it was another nurse calling to inform me that Mom had passed away at 9:30 a.m.

I thanked her for the call and walked into the kitchen. Gord's eyes filled with tears as he overheard my conversation with the nurse. He looked so sad for me, but I was determined to keep it together. I didn't even cry at first. I just stared outside, and it occurred to me that it was an absolutely beautiful day to pass away. Not only was it brilliantly sunny, it was All Saint's Day; Mom had passed away during the 9:30 a.m. Mass service. I felt numb, but I was also greatly relieved for Mom. I truly believed that she had just entered another place, one I would eventually visit. I also felt as if Mom would watch over us and ensure no harm would come to her loved ones.

Reality hit me as we drove to the hospital for the last time: Mom was gone and I would never speak or cry or laugh or hug or kiss her or sit by her bedside, ever again. She was no longer with me but somewhere else. I hoped she was happy.

When we arrived at the hospital, the first person I saw was the patient who had roomed with Mom; she had become friends with Mom in the brief time they had together. She was in a wheelchair in the hallway when she stopped me to give her condolences. She also said that it should have been her and not Mom who was so young and full of life. I hugged her.

The waiting room was full of Dad's family and my brothers. We hugged and wept on each other's shoulders. My brothers were so very close to Mom, and had supported her every step of the way in her final few months. I noticed Aunt Linda and she took my hand and led me towards Mom's room. I stopped and asked her if Mom was still there. Aunt Linda said that she was and wanted me to see her. I hesitated for a couple minutes but then Dad came out, held me, and then led me to Mom's bed. I didn't want to look at her, but once I did, it explained why they wanted me to see her. Mom wore a smile and looked so peaceful. I knew at that moment that she was in a happy place, far away from all the troubles of the world.

Dad and his family looked after the funeral arrangements. There was going to be two days of viewing with an open casket followed by a funeral service on the third day. Being Catholic, this is what Mom wanted. My only responsibility was to go to my parents home to get the outfit that Mom had told me she wanted to rest in. I did this on the same day of her passing. I cannot recall how I managed it or what thoughts went through my mind; all that has been lost to me, perhaps, due to some innate method of self protection that serves to keep us from moments of intense pain and sadness.

I felt empty inside for most of the next few days. There was something missing in me and in the world around me; a space that could never be filled. I called my boss and let him know that I wouldn't be in for a few days. He told me to take as much time as I needed. I was an absolute mess mentally and without any bearings. I told Gord that there was no way I could endure seeing Mom in a casket for three days. Just the thought made me nauseous. Gord went to our family doctor and came home with some pills to calm me. He told me to take one right away and then get dressed. I felt better after my shower. The tranquilizer kicked in, and I felt nothing. My mind was empty of any thoughts whatsoever. I changed into the new black suit that I had tailored for this specific occasion.

As soon as Gord and I arrived at the funeral home, I saw Memère Rose and my tears started to flow. I had my own pain of losing a mother, but I couldn't imagine the pain she must have felt at losing a daughter; especially one she was so close to. We walked inside together, and there was Mom, lying so peacefully in her casket, in the outfit she wished to wear. Her hair was beautifully swept up in a bun;

I've only ever remembered her wearing her hair like that. I didn't even cry. I was just relieved that she was not in any more emotional or physical pain.

There were many people coming and going. There were familiar faces as well as people I barely knew or had not seen for years; all had come to pay their respects to my family with the same look of sadness and concern. The flower arrangements were massive, and the scent that filled the room made me nauseous. Gord took me to a nearby restaurant for a break. I only had a glass of wine and a few bites of food, but I guess the mix of wine and tranquilizers helped anaesthetize me. It felt good not to have to deal with the situation.

On the day of the funeral, tears rolled continuously down my cheeks. I wore my black suit again on this horrible, yet befittingly rainy day. The service was beautiful, at least as much as I was able to grasp of it. On our way to the cemetery, my immediate family drove together in a limousine and everyone else followed behind us. I sat and watched the whole scene unfold before me. It felt as if I was watching someone else's life; the cars driving past with grieving relatives, the condolences, the flowers. It was a surreal experience and it left me feeling disjointed and upset.

It was cold with pouring rain when we arrived at the cemetery. The grave was already dug, and the priest was speaking quickly as the coffin was suspended over it. My pain was excruciating. I couldn't breathe. I just wanted to leave.

After the service, I said goodbye to Mom for one last time and took a red rose, which I planned to keep forever, off the casket.

The thought that such things happen everyday, eases the pain no less when you are in the middle of the storm. Somehow though, at the center of the storm, for a brief second, there is calm and silence - a time for remembrance and forgiveness. There were times in the days prior to Mom's death, when I had been angry with my family for keeping things from me. But I began to see it more as a final gift from Mom; something I had to do for her as well as me.

I went back to work just five days after Mom's death, because it was the only thing I could do to keep my mind occupied and my thoughts off the events of the last week; I kept busy and gradually, my pain seemed to diminish slightly with every passing day.

Christmas was quickly approaching and I knew my family wouldn't want to celebrate it. However, I was also aware that Christmas time had been Mom's favorite holiday. She would have wanted all of us to, at the very least, acknowledge the holiday together. Our whole family always celebrated on Christmas Eve, so I invited everyone to our house for dinner. My house was lit up like the fourth of July, because Gord had given me the task of hanging hundreds of lights on the windows of our house to keep me busy. Everywhere you looked, there were lights, decorations, and the happy bright trappings of the festive season.

Knowing that this day would be emotionally challenging for me I began drinking wine too early. By the dinner time, I was unable to organize the meal, and poor Gord had to take over from me; needless to say, he was not pleased with my behavior. However, the dinner was a success. After dinner I gave out a few presents. Nobody was supposed to buy gifts, but I gave a present to Dad and my grandparents. When they opened it, tears trickled down both my grandparents' cheeks. It was a black and white photograph of Mom when she was strikingly beautiful at twenty-two years old; it was a close up of her where her eyes appeared to be staring right back at you. I had the photo enlarged and placed in an antique-looking pewter frame. They all thanked me for the present and promised to cherish it forever.

When everyone had left, I felt overjoyed that I had made it possible, with Gord's help, for my family to be assembled together. It could have been the worst Christmas ever with everyone staying home and mourning Mom's death. I thought we could celebrate her life. I felt that Mom was up in heaven looking down on her family on that day. I went to bed that night, secretly wishing Mom a Merry Christmas and telling her how much I loved and missed her.

The world seemed a different place now. Not only was I now missing a mother in my life; I also had two sisters out there somewhere. I thought of my sisters often and talked about them to Tina and Memère Rose. We wondered what they looked like, what their names were, whether they had families of their own, and all the other small but significant things that go into making someone's life.

When I confided in Memère Rose about my two sisters, I could tell that she was surprised yet very happy that it was finally out in the open. She didn't seem surprised that Aunt Linda was the one who exposed the truth but was thankful that we didn't discuss it with Mom before she passed away. However, Memère Rose was surprised that Mom spoke of them before passing since she never spoke to Memère Rose about them. I had many questions for Memère Rose, but at that moment I just wanted her to know that Tina and I both knew and would one day search for these two sisters.

My life went on and the days seemed to fly by. Gord started his own company early in 1993. I wasn't as supportive as I could have been because of all the things that had happened in my life. With all the negative occurrences in our lives during the past couple of years, I was not able to have as positive an outlook on life as Gord. I thanked God for giving Gord the courage and strength he required to begin a business venture at this point in our lives. I kept my job but in the evenings and on weekends, I helped Gord out with the paperwork. Only a few months had passed since Gord had started his company when another tragedy struck his family.

Gord's brother, Brian, suddenly died of AIDS at the young age of thirty-eight. I don't know how Brian had kept his illness a secret from those he loved. His passing was a shock to us all, especially his eleven year old son. My heart ached so badly for Gord and his family. I was also in pain since Brian and I were very close; he usually confided in me about everything. Unfortunately, he had felt as if he couldn't share the truth of his condition with me. On numerous occasions, I had asked him if he was feeling all right since he didn't look well, but he always responded that it was just stress.

Once again, we had to attend a heart-wrenching funeral. It didn't seem fair that Gord and I had to endure so much pain in just three short years. When was this going to stop?

We greeted all the friends and family and did the typical funeral activities. Quite a few of Brian's colleagues from IBM attended the funeral. We found out from them, that at the time of Brian's death, 6:30 am on the 11th of August, all the computers and phone lines in the building where he worked had gone down. This explained why Gord's father couldn't get through to Brian's boss to inform him of Brian's passing. We also learned that a power failure of such magnitude had never occurred at that building before, and that Brian's computer had strangely been the last to come back on.

The funeral service was short but special. All we wanted to do was get back home to grieve without so many people around us. Gord and I came to the realization that we had lost the most important people in our lives. The family members we were closest to and had spent the most time with were now gone. What could possibly hurt us now? There was also an irony to the three deaths: Gord's mother died on the 5th of May, 1991 aged 58, Mom died on 1st of November, 1992 aged

48 and Brian died on the 11th of August, 1993 aged 38. Needless to say, I was terrified about turning 28.

There was so much sadness in those years with so many people gone; it all seemed so senseless. I looked around me one day and saw so many spaces left by people I loved dearly. It would have been easier not to care in such situations; to turn off and forget things by medicating and removing myself from the world, but I wanted to create something new; something fresh that would mean a new beginning instead of an end.

I had already spoken to Tina, Memère Rose and my brothers about our adopted sisters, and now I wanted to speak to Dad about it. It was time to let Dad know that I had found out the secret that my parents thought would never be revealed.

I finally gained enough courage one Sunday morning and picked up the phone to dial Dad's number. Dad was completely shocked that we knew and demanded to know who told us. Presumably, he wanted to know if Mom discussed it with us before she died. I told him how I found out and he became extremely emotional. I assured him that we never discussed it with Mom, which seemed to ease his mind. He explained the circumstances and reasons for the adoptions; it was a repeat of what Memère Rose had said, and I felt better that they were not conflicting stories. At least I didn't have to decipher what was true and what wasn't.

I told him that I wanted to search for my sisters and he grew very silent. Dad didn't argue with my decision, but I don't think he took me seriously. I don't think he ever dreamed that we would actually find them.

3.
MY SEARCH BEGINS

In January 1996, I received a letter of reply from the Catholic Children's Aid Society (CCAS) enclosed with forms to be filled and returned. The next step was to register with the Ontario Adoption Disclosure Registry, as well as with the CCAS. I filled out all the necessary documentation and mailed it immediately.

I hated the months of waiting that followed. I checked the mailbox everyday, but nothing came. I almost gave up. However, in November of that year, I received a letter from CCAS indicating that they had received my request for non-identifying information. The letter also stated that I would be receiving this information within the next 3 or 4 months, which is the regular waiting period for priority requests.

Another Christmas went by without our late family members present, but Gord and I made the most of it once again. On the 10th of January, 1997, a whole year after I had written my first letter, I finally received a package from CCAS. I held it in my trembling hands knowing it to be the non-identifying information that I had requested. Suddenly, I felt scared, as I didn't know what kind of things would be revealed to me. With my emotions on overdrive, I decided to wait until Gord was home before opening the envelope. Thankfully, it was only minutes before Gord and I were sitting together at the kitchen table.

My heart was racing as I began to open the large envelope. I was finally going to have some information on my adopted sisters. I assumed that this information would make my sisters seem more real and closer to me. I had no idea what was inside it but I knew it was going to change my life forever.

The first thing I noticed was that each sister had four pages of information stapled together. There was a boxed heading on each set of papers; one heading read "Half-Sister," while the other read "Full Sister." I had no idea what this meant, because as far as I knew, both my sisters were born to my parents. At least, I had taken that to be the truth from what Aunt Linda said.

I read the document headed "Half Sister" first, as I assumed this to be a mistake. It placed my sister's birth year in 1964 and her place of birth at the Toronto General Hospital. Her racial origins were Caucasian and her ethnic origins were French and unknown. It then struck me that they could not have known about Dad's Italian heritage, which is why they had headed her paper "Half Sister." I was a little relieved to realize this and read on; the labor had lasted twelve hours and the baby's birth weight was 6 lbs and 15.5 ozs. At six months of age, she was described as being, "a very pale, thin, and delicate looking baby." The paper went on to detail that she had large blue eyes, brown hair and a fair complexion. She was under the care of the Metro Children's Aid Society at birth, and remained in a society foster home until her adoption at the age of ten months.

The paper also detailed the profile of the adoptive parents. The mother was, it said, in her early thirties at the time of adoption, with striking black hair and grey eyes, and was of English and Scottish origin. She was described as a capable and well organized woman who enjoyed being a wife and mother.

The father was in his late thirties, Irish Roman Catholic, of average height with very dark brown hair and blue-green eyes. He was university educated and self-employed in a professional field. The adoptive parents had been married for ten years and had another adopted child, a son aged four.

All this seemed so positive and, as I read, I felt glad that my sister had found a family that was stable and secure and could love her as she deserved. Her adoptive parents seemed, at least on paper, to be friendly, mature, well educated, and professional. I imagined them as a family group, like the picture taken while my sister was still a baby; her adoptive mother with her striking good looks, holding her in her arms, and her adoptive father, in his early thirties with dark brown hair, staring into the camera with a kind of assured maturity.

I turned over the page and began to read about my other sister.

She was born in 1963 at the Women's College Hospital, Ontario. They had correctly listed her origins as French and Italian and of having been admitted to the Society at 2 weeks of age. Her birth weight was 7 lbs and half an ounce. She was described as an attractive newborn with "reddish brown hair, blue eyes and a fair complexion".

She was said to be an alert and cuddly baby who suffered from a number of infant conditions, none of which were serious.

At two months of age, she was placed with her adoptive family. Her adoption was finalized when she was approximately nine months old; her adoptive mother was in her early thirties, of Irish Catholic heritage and was trained as a nurse's assistant firstly, then as a technician in the field of health care. She was a full time mother at the time of the adoption. My sister's adoptive father was almost thirty; tall, with brown hair and a slight build and was working as a technician in the health care field. They had been married for four years and lived in Toronto at the time of the adoption.

I must have read the information a dozen times before I finally broke down. Reality had set in; I had two sisters out there, presently in their mid-thirties who had not registered an interest to meet their birth family because they didn't want to be found. I felt that this might be all I would ever know of them. I also couldn't help but feel sad for Mom. She had carried these babies for nine long months, enough time for her to bond with them, only to be forced to give them away. Mom would have been pleased to hear they were in good health and were adopted by families who seemed to be good, loving people.

After repeatedly reading the information for a couple more hours, I couldn't wait to call Tina and read it out to her. My voice was shaky as I read her all the information. I knew she had tears in her eyes on the other end of the line. Tina made similar conclusions to mine about the adoptive parents. We both just hoped that our unknown sisters had a good life and that they would some day want to meet their birth family.

After hanging up with Tina, I called Memère Rose and gave her all the information. She was elated to hear the details and said that she had prayed for years that the two girls would be placed in good homes. Memère Rose then began to tell me the story of why she would not allow Mom to keep the babies. I knew the story already, having confirmed it with Dad, but it made Memère Rose feel better to know that I had accepted her reasons, or at least, understood them.

I let Memère Rose talk for quite some time before I asked her why the second baby's papers, the one headed "Half Sister," hadn't listed Dad's ethnic origin. Memère Rose explained that she was indeed my full sister but Mom was so embarrassed that it happened twice, that she gave false information about the birth father. I accepted her explanation for the meantime, but decided that I would one day ask Dad as well.

The papers had put flesh on the bones of my sisters who, up until that point, had been merely shadows on the walls. I still did not know their names or their faces, but they were more human now, born out of the scraps of information that sat in a drawer somewhere, waiting for me to come along and find. There were thousands, perhaps, millions of other files like these in the world. It amazed me that these files had found their way to me or even that it could mean so much. I read over them again for what seemed like the hundredth time, taking in every detail; wanting to create them, bit by bit.

I couldn't stop asking myself questions about my two sisters; who were they? What did they look like? What were their names? Every time I saw a girl of the right age on the street, with a passing resemblance to my family, I thought to myself: is she the one? Is she one of the sisters I have lost?

In the latter part of 1997, I went with Tina to see a fortune teller. Tina had her fortune read first but did not ask any questions. When it was my turn, I tape-recorded the session. The first half of the session went well and the fortune teller revealed quite a few correct facts. So, when the time came for me to ask questions, I asked about my "lost sisters". She told me that the baby Mom had held for a brief moment, lived close by, while the other one lived very far away. I asked her if I would someday meet one or both of them, and she said that I would certainly meet the sister who lived close by. It felt odd to be hearing this from a stranger but I took the news at face value without allowing myself to get my hopes up.

Wherever they were, the papers had brought my sisters a little closer to me. I may not have known everything about them, but I felt as though I knew them as babies. I knew about their weight at birth, their illnesses, their adoptive parents, and whether they were carried to the full term or not. Gradually, bit by bit, my sisters were being revealed to me.

4.
A MATCH

It was May of 1998 and I was at work with Gord. We had some of our sub-contractors in our office, and it was loud and busy as usual. My phone rang, and I answered it as I covered one of my ears with my other hand to mute the background noise. A lady introduced herself to me as Lina. She said she was calling from the Catholic Children's Aid Society, so I asked her to hold as I requested everyone, with the exception of Gord, to leave our office.

I took Lina off hold and apologized for the wait. She asked me if I was still interested in finding my sisters. Without hesitation I answered, "Absolutely!" That's when Lina told me that one of the two girls had registered. I could not believe it, and I started crying, unable to speak. I just held out the receiver to Gord who had been listening to my side of the conversation. He took the phone and jokingly told Lina that I was a tad emotional with whatever she had just told me.

I composed myself as best I could in order to continue my conversation with Lina. I apologized, and she reassured me that my reaction wasn't uncommon. I asked Lina what would happen next. She said she would contact my sister and make sure that she was still interested in meeting her birth family. Lina was certain that she was since she had just very recently registered. Once Lina made contact with my new found sister, we could write letters to one another and send photos, or whatever we both agreed to. Lina indicated that we could both take this as slowly or as quickly as we wanted. I asked which sister this was and found out that it was the second girl.

Just prior to hanging up the phone, it dawned on me that I didn't know for sure what my sister's name was. Unfortunately, Lina couldn't give me that information quite yet, but said that she would refer to my sister as Lisa, the name Mom had given her.

That evening, I called Tina to give her the great news, and she was as shocked and excited as I was about the prospect of meeting one of our sisters. It was unbelievable to both of us that one of them registered only a year after I did. I told her everything that Lina said on the phone, and we discussed what we thought we should do next. Of course, neither of us knew what we could or should do, so we decided to just wait and see what would happen in the next few days.

I called Memère Rose the next day to let her know that one of the girls had registered, and she was almost in tears with happiness. Memère Rose's dream was to one day, meet one or both of her granddaughters who she had regrettably insisted be given away for adoption. Just the sound of Memère Rose's voice made me want to give her what she wished for. I felt we were closer than we had ever been in our entire lives.

A few days went by, and I didn't hear back from Lina or anyone at the CCAS. My concern was growing steadily. Finally, I couldn't stand to wait any longer and I called her. Lina informed me that she had called my sister at work a couple of times. She left a message the first time, and the second time she was told that my sister no longer worked there. I was disappointed with this news. I was so anxious to meet my sister but there was nothing I could do, except try to be patient and await Lina's call back.

Another week went by, and I still heard nothing. I couldn't wait any longer so I phoned Lina again and asked her about the progress of the search for my sister. I had created all kinds of crazy scenarios about my sister being a waitress at a bar or even an exotic dancer because, in one of our phone calls, Lina mentioned that my sister's workplace was almost too loud to leave a message. My mind started playing tricks on me because of my frustration at Lina's unsuccessful attempts at contacting my sister. We had come so close and now the agency couldn't reach her.

It was nearing the end of July, almost two months since my first phone call from Lina informing me that my sister had registered. Where was she? Was she getting her messages? Why did she register if she never really wanted to be found? These were all the questions that were racing through my mind. I wanted them answered so badly.

I could not think what the hold up was. Then it hit me, perhaps my sister didn't want us to contact her after all; perhaps she had changed her mind and wanted to remain apart from us. That thought was almost too depressing for me to bear. I could not face the idea that after all the effort and sadness, it had come to nothing in the final stages.

Another few days passed before Lina called me at work. She said she must discontinue her attempts at reaching my sister because leaving any more messages could be misconstrued as harassment. She regretted to inform me that this case was over for the agency and that I would have to search for my sister, myself. Naturally, I was devastated and desperately asked her what other avenue I should take. Lina said she was closing the file today and would be mailing me a list of private investigators that I could employ to attempt to locate my sister based on the little information I had. Lina's hands were tied, and I respected her position and thanked her for her efforts. I told Gord and Tina the news, and they were both as disappointed as I was. But one fact remained; my sister had registered only a few months ago indicating her desire to meet her birth family. Surely, this was something to hold on to, something to pin our hopes to.

I tidied up my desk and left the office. As I arrived home, all I wanted to do was cry with frustration. I had come so far and so many things had gone right; how could this go wrong now? I put my keys on the table and glanced across at the phone, only to notice that there was a message waiting. I quickly crossed the room and played back the message. I immediately recognized Lina's voice. She sounded excited and asked to call her as soon as possible. Luckily, her number was on speed dial so I just had to press one key while my hands were shaking nervously. Lina's message indicated that she was leaving her office at 4 p.m. and said to call her before then. It was 3:50 p.m. I hoped she hadn't left early. There was no way I would have been able to wait any longer to hear what Lina had to say.

The phone rang twice, and Lina answered on the third ring. I didn't even wait for her to finish saying her last name when I blurted out, "It's Debbie, what's happening?" At this point I had no idea why she was calling me, considering that she said she was closing my file earlier that day; but I was hoping for the best. Lina spoke excitedly and told me that she had finally talked with my adopted sister, Lisa, who was overjoyed to discover she had birth relatives. I was utterly shocked and before I could ask her how this happened, she told me that before she closed the file she had decided to make one last attempt at contacting Lisa and had succeeded in finally reaching her. My heart was pounding and my eyes filled with tears. The day had gone from sadness to extreme joy in just a few short hours.

I managed to ask Lina why it had been so difficult to reach my sister. She said Lisa had just been laid off work at a factory, which explained the noise and the communication problems. However, the main reason Lisa had not returned Lina's messages at home was because she had received a letter from her local Children's Aid Society informing her that her birth mother was deceased. The letter never mentioned that another birth family member had registered. So Lisa had assumed that Lina was calling to give her this same devastating information.

I questioned Lina as to why such a letter would be sent to Lisa in such poor taste and with absolutely no compassion. Lina agreed with me and said she was extremely upset when hearing this news herself. She assured me that she would look into it, but we didn't labor the point. All I wanted to hear was my sister's reaction to the news that I was searching for her, and that she had birth brothers, sisters, a father, grandparents and other extended family members. Lina said that my sister was crying over the phone with joy. Unfortunately, Lisa had believed that her recent registration had resulted only in pain; that any hopes of ever meeting a birth relative had vanished. Lisa never dreamt that her birth mother and father would have married and had two more girls and two boys. Lisa was also made aware that she had an older sister who had been given away for adoption before her.

The connection had been made between us and somehow, I felt things were different at last; finally, things were moving forward. Lina said that Lisa wanted to meet me but that she also needed time to get used to the news. I felt that I did too. This was something momentous in both our lives, and we wanted to get things right and have everything in place. Lina then told me that she could tell me Lisa's given first name; it was Maureen. We had only used Lisa, because it was the name Mom had given her at birth.

Maureen had lived in Oshawa, Ontario her entire life. I was so surprised by this information. Our family only lived half an hour away from Oshawa, so for all we knew, one of us may have bumped into her at some point in our lives. Lina also mentioned a little more about Maureen's family life; Maureen's parents had adopted a boy before adopting her and later they had conceived a girl. I was also told that Maureen left home at a very young age.

The news left me feeling elated and happy for the first time in years, but I still felt as though I did not want things to happen too quickly. I had waited so long for this moment, and I did not want anything to spoil it. So both Maureen and I agreed on writing to one another at first, and we'd take the rest from there. I told Lina that I would write to Maureen first and then wait for a return letter. Lina agreed that it made sense for me to make the initial contact since Maureen seemed very emotionally fragile; I hoped I could answer some of her long awaited questions.

I had to send my letter to Lina and have her forward it to Maureen since I was not yet allowed to have Maureen's mailing address. Basically, the only information I could have about Maureen at that point was her first name, the town she resided in, that she was married, and that she had a very young daughter. Maureen was real now, and I couldn't wait to tell Tina and Gord about this unreal news.

Neither of them could believe it, as it was only that same day that I had told them the file on my missing sister had been closed; that I had virtually no hope now of finding her. For one of my sisters, at least, the search was over. I also knew, however, that in many ways the process had only just begun. I still had to summon up the courage and the presence of mind to write to her. That evening, my mind was overflowing with things to include in this letter. There was so much to tell her, but I didn't want to scare her away either. I was just so thrilled at the prospect of meeting her soon.

On the 28th of July, 1998, I sat outside in my deck chair with a blank sheet of paper in front of me and stared. At first nothing came to mind; I thought about Mom and Dad, and how much to tell Maureen about them. How much do I say about my own childhood? Do I tell her how much I know about the situation surrounding her adoption? I did not know what to write, but I took a deep breath, put my pen to the paper, and began:

28 July 98

Dear Maureen,

How do I begin this letter? I'm sure you'll have as much confusion, anxiousness, and so on, as I'm feeling at this moment. I've read the "guidelines" in the kit Lina sent me and have had many of my friends and family comment on what to include in this letter, but I'm just going to write what I'm feeling and what I think could answer some of your questions.

I found out about you around six years ago; in fact, it was 3 weeks before Mom's (your birth mother's) death. Mom's sister told me because she feared that Mom would start talking about the babies in front of us, and that we wouldn't know what she was talking about. We never did discuss nor admit that we knew because, for some reason, Mom and Dad (your birth father) wanted to keep it a secret. I respected Mom's wishes. However, Mom was apparently talking to her sister a great deal before she passed away about the two girls she had to give up for adoption. We will never know exactly what Mom's thoughts were all these years, but somehow I feel like she never really let one day pass by without thinking back.

The story of why Mom and Dad were forced into giving you up is very long, but I will try to simplify it. There were two baby girls given up for adoption; the sister born in 1963 (still unknown, she has yet to register), then you in 1964. Mom was living with her mother and little sister at that time. Her father was in the hospital with Multiple Sclerosis and had been for quite some time. Her mother was also having some bad health problems and was in and out of the hospital after undergoing many intestinal operations. Her sister was eleven years younger than she was, and she had to take care of her. Mom was also needed to contribute financially to the household. Anyway, Dad did ask Mom to marry him in both circumstances. But as much as Mom wanted that, grandmother could not let Mom leave the house and move on with her own life. Mom was needed at her parent's home more than we could ever imagine. I have spoken to both grandmother and Dad about the circumstances and they both told me the same story. I hope one day for you to hear about the story in person.

In 1965, our parents married and had a baby girl they named Tina; Tina is now married and has a precious little girl, Shanelle Nicole, who is six. They live close to me and we see them quite regularly. I feel very close to Tina, even though we are quite different. Currently, Tina is separated from her husband of 12 years, but who knows?

In 1967, Mom's father passed away with Multiple Sclerosis. I was born in October of that year. As you know, my name is Debbie and I have a somewhat similar life to you. I left home at 17 and found my own apartment and job. At 18, I met a man at work who was 16 years my senior and we became friends. At 19, we started dating and at 21, we were married. We are married to this day and will be celebrating our 10 year wedding anniversary this November.

In 1969, Mom and Dad had their first baby boy. They named him Leonard Andrew, after Dad's Italian father, Leonardo. Lenny has recently moved to Pickering with a friend and is not involved in a relationship at this time. He's already finished his schooling and will be a Chartered Accountant in 2 years.

In 1971, my parents had another baby boy that they named Rocky, after Dad's name, Rocco. Rocky lives in downtown Toronto and is single. He is a graphic designer.

And that's it for brothers and sisters. I apologize if I've overwhelmed you.

I don't know what information you've been given about your birth mother and father so I'll brief you.

Mom was French Canadian, born in Welland, but raised in Toronto. She only had one sister named Linda, as I mentioned, who was 11 years younger. Mom worked in a mailroom as a supervisor for most of her married life and while she was raising us. There's so much to tell you, and I will when we hopefully meet. All I can say is that she was the most wonderful mother and person I will ever know. Her sudden death, from cancer, was just not fair. We all grieved her and always will, forever, but she left us with so many wonderful memories. I have to look at some of the positive things that have occurred since her death; most of all, knowing about you and now, having the opportunity to meet you. I believe that she somehow has been instrumental in the meeting of one another.

Dad is Italian, and his family came to Canada when he was 14. I'm getting sidetracked, but I must mention that in the information I was provided about you, it had listed "father" as "unknown." Apparently, Mom didn't provide Dad's name because this was the second baby she was giving up for adoption, and she was embarrassed and frightened. I have spoken to Dad and he says he is, without question, your birth father. Dad was a business man and unfortunately, was not home very often (during daylight hours anyways). We never really got very close to him and to this day, I see him about twice a year. He has not remarried since Mom's death, and I doubt he ever will. He has two brothers and one sister. His parents are still alive; in fact, they will be celebrating their 60th wedding anniversary next year. They are super people who loved Mom so much. Dad lives in Scarborough with his brother.

Mom's mother, our grandmother, remarried after the death of her husband and we are very close to her. She was a second mother to us when we were growing up. In fact, our family lived with her and Leandre (her second husband) for the first 11 years of my life. Her name is Rose and what an appropriate name. She is so beautiful and *almost superhuman. She and Mom were the closest a mother and daughter could ever be. Her life is so full of history that I know she can't wait to tell you. We call her Memère, French for grandmother. We are all still very close to her and I try to spend at least 3 weekends a year with her and Leandre (she lives 2 hours from me).*

So, that's the brief on the family and my writing seems to be getting worse. By the way, I haven't hand written in God knows, 10 years. I'm always on the computer.

Now, for some fun personal stuff! I'm sure you have wondered, as I have, if we look alike? I'm 5'3", 120 pounds with grey eyes and long, curly, dark brown hair with auburn highlights. I stay fit by weight training, and I have enjoyed good health.

Tina is 5'6" and very slim with green eyes. Lenny is 5'8" with big blue eyes, and Rocky is 6'0" with blue/green eyes. Mom had almost purple eyes, like Elizabeth Taylor, and Dad has lime green eyes. Even Dad's Italian parents have blue and green eyes, probably because they're from South-Central Italy. We all have dark hair, but it is not necessarily real (some of us have quite a bit of grey – ME!).

I live with my husband, Gord, in Aurora, and we work together in Mississauga. We have a great relationship, and I couldn't have dreamt for a better husband. We don't have children and probably won't since he was "fixed" over 15 years ago. We have nephews and a niece to keep us busy.

I heard that you're married with a little girl who's 16 months old. That's great, and I hope to meet the three of you one day soon!

The information I received about your adoptive parents seemed good. I hope your family gave you the love and support you required to live a happy childhood. I can't wait to hear about your life growing up, and what it's like today! I understand you have an older adopted brother and a little sister as well. Can't wait to hear about them too.

After all this information, I hope you realize that there is so much more to tell you. I would like the chance to meet with you face to face. I want to do this your way, and as slowly or as quickly as you feel comfortable with. Don't worry, I wouldn't have you attend a family reunion as a mystery guest or anything (ha! ha!).

I just want you to know there are family members that would really like to meet you and know you. To what extent, I don't exactly know, but I can tell you that I would like to meet you and hopefully become friends.

I understand your husband encouraged you to register and coincidentally so did mine. Since we both have such supportive husbands maybe it would be a good idea for the four of us to meet for the first time at a place that's convenient for you.

In closing, I'm looking forward to receiving your letter soon and meeting some day soon.

Your birth sister,

Debbie

I sat back and read my letter aloud to Gord who listened intently. It was finished, and I could hardly believe I was at this point. The person I had thought about so much for the past months, the person I thought I was never going to see, was almost within reach. I mailed the letter to Lina at CCAS the following day. I heard it hit the bottom of the mailbox and wished it good luck.

I decided not to include photographs quite yet for fear that if Maureen had a letter with photos then that may be enough information for her, and she would end her search. I was feeling a little insecure. I felt like I was walking on thin ice with Maureen since it took so long to make contact with her. And just as Lina had instructed, my letter also did not divulge any identifying information. Lina told me that I should call her back after Maureen wrote me a responding letter. There would be a waiver for me to sign; one giving Lina permission to tell Maureen my phone number and any other personal information. For some reason, I felt my sister would be very delicate, emotionally, so I decided to try and take things at her pace and use caution when communicating.

The threads that connected us were so thin I felt as though they might break at any second; like the delicate weave of a spider's web that seems so strong and yet was so weak at the same time. Lina said she would contact me as soon as she received a letter from Maureen. She would then courier or mail the letter to me; whichever I wished.

A few weeks passed and I still had not heard from Lina. Of course, I became anxious. Things started to occur to me: What if the letter had been too forward? What if my sister had been frightened off? What if…what if…?

I called the Society to find out if something had gone horribly wrong. Lina said that she hadn't received a letter yet but to relax and be patient. There was a lot of information for Maureen to digest; therefore, she might take a while to respond. Even though everything Lina said made sense I couldn't help but be disappointed that Maureen hadn't communicated with me immediately. Once again, my expectations were unrealistic since I had no idea what it was like to be in Maureen's shoes. Maureen was the one who was the adoptee and had just found out about all these siblings who were her full blood.

I waited and waited but still, nothing. Everyday I rushed to see if there was a letter waiting, but everyday it was the same; nothing. I called Lina and she told me that there was no word from Maureen and that this kind of thing happened all the time. But it did not seem to pacify me; I felt disenchanted and disappointed. More questions came to mind; was the letter too overwhelming for Maureen? Worse, did the letter have all the information Maureen wanted and needed? Did she change her mind about wanting to meet her birth family? And the biggest question of all - had she only ever wanted to meet her birth mother?

I must admit I became a little obsessed with wanting to meet my birth sister; it occupied my thoughts every waking moment, and began to affect my way of thinking. Fortunately, my family and friends were strong and supportive enough to help me through it. It had been over two months since I had written to Maureen, and I still heard nothing. I had waited for some news; just a note, or perhaps a word, or a sign that she was as eager to meet me as I was to meet her. There was however, nothing. The ball was firmly in Maureen's court.

October began and my birthday came and went, but still, I heard no word. Then it happened: Lina called and said that she had finally received a letter addressed to me from Maureen. I was almost in too much shock to be excited. It was Friday, and I knew the weekend would seem extra long in anticipation of Maureen's letter. I couldn't wait to find out why it had taken her ages to respond. It took such a long time for Lina to contact Maureen to let her know that there was a match, and now it took equally as long for Maureen to respond to my letter. Hopefully, this was something Maureen still really wanted.

It was Tuesday afternoon when I picked up the mail from the centralized mailboxes. There was an envelope from CCAS, and I knew it was the long awaited letter from my sister, Maureen. My hands were shaking as I drove home. I ran out of the car and into the house where Gord was waiting for me. I told him about the envelope, and he was thrilled that it had finally arrived. Gord insisted that I not waste anymore time and to hurry up and open it.

I breathed deeply for a second and let the moment wash over me. Somehow, I could not believe that it was finally here. I barely managed to open the envelope; my hands were trembling so much. First, I noticed how beautiful Maureen's handwriting was and then how short of a letter it was; only two pages. I felt a twinge of disappointment due to the shortness of the letter, but I pushed the feeling aside. I held the letter in front of me and began to read:

18 October 1998

Dear Debbie,

I would like to start this letter by saying how very sorry I am for not writing back to you sooner. I'm hoping you haven't given up on me or changed your mind about wanting to get to know each other more in time. I was very excited to receive your letter and find out about my "other family." The passing away of your mother (my birth mother) was a great shock to me, and there have been many thoughts and feelings going through me since then. I'm very sorry to hear that you lost your mother. I was so looking forward to meeting her, but I'm sure you have lots of great memories and pictures to share with me, if you will. I've wanted to register since I was a teenager but never really got the courage to do it. My husband helped me understand that it would be good for me to do the search and know where I came from. I'll have to be honest with you, for years it seemed like there was a part of me missing, and it was hard for me to know why I am the way I am. Hopefully things will now come together, and I can see better the person inside.

There really isn't much to tell you about my family because we are not close. My parents don't talk, or come over to see me much, and it has pretty well been that way all my life. They provided for me, but there was not much love and affection shown. I have an older brother, Michael, who was also adopted, but my parents had a hard time raising him. I think that's why they were much stricter with me. My mother was told she couldn't have children and then was surprised when she got pregnant at 40 with my sister Tara. Things changed not long after she was home, and I could not understand why it happened. I haven't seen my brother in over 10 years. My sister very rarely comes over or calls. It's been hard not having much of a family life, but I've seemed to come to terms with it and got on with my own life.

Enough of the depressing stuff, now I'll tell you a bit about my own family and myself. I'm 34, 5'2". I have auburn colored hair (not my natural color if you know what I mean!) and my eyes are green. I'm a little bit on the overweight side, but I'm working on that now. It doesn't help being short and all. I enjoy the outdoors very much and like to go camping, fishing, boating, hiking and just sitting by an open fire in the cool air. We are very active in dart leagues as well and I've started bowling again.

My husband Paul is 36, 5'10" and husky in build with red hair. He's a great guy with a great sense of humor. He is always doing and saying crazy things. I think that's what attracted me most to him. We met 11 years ago at a factory in Ajax and have been together ever since. We married in 1994 and started a family in 1997. Megan was born on 3 April 1997, exactly, on my due date. She has brought great joy and keeps us on our toes too! She has a very bubbly personality and is always doing crazy things. I think she takes after her dad in every way but some people say she looks more like me. We both work opposite shifts so we don't get to spend much time with Megan during the week. Of course, we make up for it on the weekends.

Well, I know this letter may seem kind of short to you, but I find it very hard to express my feelings on paper. This definitely was one of the hardest things I've ever had to do. Again, I hope you can forgive me for not writing back much sooner. There have been a lot of things happening in my life lately, and it has taken awhile to sort everything out. I am very excited about finding out that I have more sisters and brothers. I hope some day to meet everyone. I have no living grandparents now so it would be nice to meet your grandparents as well, if they want to. I'm looking forward to hearing from you again, and I would very much like for us to get together some time soon if you'd like.

Maureen

After reading the letter, I couldn't help but cry. I was so thankful that she was still interested in meeting my family. I had doubted if Maureen wanted to meet her birth family at all, but here, I had the proof that she was just as anxious as we were to reunite the two parts that had been separated for so long.

I read the letter again and again; its words both thrilled and chilled me; it was like looking into the mouth of a new life. The news of her family made me anxious. I could not bear to think of my sister without a family and was determined that I would give her the thing that she so obviously needed, even though she said she didn't.

I was very happy to hear that I had another niece. I realized the significance of my niece's birth date, 3rd April, at once; it was my parents wedding anniversary!

I couldn't wait to tell Maureen, knowing that she would find this a fascinating revelation. It was obvious from the letter that she was a sensitive and emotional girl, not that dissimilar to me. Lina was correct in her analysis of Maureen and so, I decided to let Maureen make the next move.

I decided I would call Lina at CCAS the next morning to find out what the next step was. But first, I called Tina and read Maureen's letter to her. She was thrilled that we were now communicating, and it would only be a matter of time before we met our sister. It felt good to both of us that we now knew a little bit about Maureen. It certainly was a start.

I told Lina that I had read Maureen's letter, and that I desperately wanted to take things further with my sister. I mentioned that Maureen's letter indicated that she didn't like to express her feelings on paper and would like to get together with us soon. Lina agreed that letter writing was a slow process. She said she would fax us both a waiver form to sign and fax back to her since it sounded like we were both ready to take it to the next level. The waiver allowed the agency to give personal information to the both of us. I signed it immediately and faxed it back to the agency. Lina called me a couple of hours later and said that she had spoken with Maureen and had given her my phone number. However, Maureen had wanted Lina to give me her number and asked if I could make the first call instead.

I looked at the little slip of paper with Maureen's phone number on it, and I couldn't help but break down. I could not believe that my sister was only a phone call away. All the months of waiting, all the hours spent wishing something would happen had come to this; a tiny moment in the lives of two people, but one that meant everything to us. The numbers somehow took on a magical quality; as if, they were going to change my life. I stared at the numbers in my hands and waited for a while, thinking about what I was going to say.

I was instructed by Lina to call Maureen after 9 p.m. during the week and at any time during the weekend. Curiosity got the better of me and the next morning, thinking Maureen and her husband would be at work, I called the number. After two rings, a man answered, which took me by surprise and I hung up. I felt embarrassed, but it didn't feel right speaking with someone whom I assumed was her husband, before speaking with Maureen. It occurred to me that in her letter, Maureen had indicated that she and her husband worked opposite shifts; I had completely forgotten. I guess he worked nights and slept all day. Part of me wanted to call back and apologize, but I decided to admit what I did when I spoke with Maureen instead. It was Thursday and I decided to call Maureen the next night.

At exactly 9 p.m. on Friday, I called Maureen's number and again, a man answered. I asked for Maureen, and he told me to hold for a moment. My heart was pounding and my throat was already parched. A woman came on the line and just said, "Hello?" I told her who I was and asked how she was doing. She said she was fine and asked me the same. I admitted to being nervous and anxious. She admitted to feeling the same way. We talked about our letters to one another and then she asked me, with a very shaky voice, the question I was dreading, "Did Mom ever think about me?" I explained that I had never discussed the adoptions with Mom, but that when Mom was dying, she had apparently spoken about the babies she had given away.

I expressed to Maureen that I was sure that Mom had thought about her first two babies all the time. I mentioned her love for her children and reiterated that the adoption wasn't Mom's wish. Then Maureen inquired about Mom's illness. I began to cry as I talked about Mom's last few months. The memories were very painful for me, and talking about them with the girl Mom had given birth to, but had never known, just broke my heart. Maureen began crying as well. She said, she had wanted to meet her birth mother so badly and was devastated when she heard that she was dead. I guess, never feeling close to the mother who raised her, made her want to feel close to her birth mother instead. I told Maureen I would tell her as much as I can remember about Mom and even give her some pictures. But I added that she would have to accept the fact that she would only ever meet her siblings, her grandparents on Mom's side, and maybe her birth father. She seemed very happy to hear about her birth family and all the siblings she had.

We spoke for a while before I asked when, where and how she wanted to meet for the first time. Maureen shared her feelings about only wanting to meet one family member at a time, since this was all so overwhelming for her. She suggested that she and her husband, Paul, could meet Gord and I at a restaurant. Without hesitation, I agreed and suggested we meet at a central location to both our homes. I recommended a restaurant called Santos, in the city of Scarborough. Gord and I knew the owners, and my parents had their 25th wedding anniversary dinner party there. She asked me if it was fancy and said that she didn't own a lot of dressy clothes since her job was not conducive to nice clothes. I assured her that she could wear whatever she liked and that Gord and I would be wearing jeans. I also told her that we would be picking up the tab; I didn't want Maureen to feel any additional pressure as the stress of meeting one of her birth siblings for the first time was taxing enough. We agreed to meet on the Saturday of the next weekend. I promised her I would be in touch before then.

A few days after our initial conversation, I called to speak with Maureen again. We began feeling more comfortable with each other and started talking about sisterly things like our height, our weight, our breast size, and so on. It sounded like we had similar hair color, bottled color that is, and we were basically the same height. Maureen was a little heavier than I was after the birth of her daughter, but was looking to lose a few pounds.

I told Maureen about her daughter's birthday being on our parents wedding anniversary. She was taken aback and said, "That's spooky." It was extremely coincidental that her daughter was scheduled to be delivered and had in fact arrived into this world on the 3rd of April.

We spoke about my brothers and sister and my relationship with them. I disclosed that I was closest to Tina and her daughter Shanelle, but that I did love my brothers although I didn't see them all that often. I told Maureen that Tina, like me, was anxious to meet her "older sister." Maureen and I continued our conversation for some time, and then I told her I would call her on Saturday morning before meeting in person.

For the next few days, I walked about as if in a dream. Nothing seemed to make sense but it all seemed wonderfully right somehow; my sister was closer than I had ever felt her before, and in a few short days, I was going to meet her. I imagined all kinds of things: what the meal would be like; what my sister's husband would be like; would my sister look like Mom or me? It was such a relief to have come this far, and I was hungry for more; I wanted to take all I could from the experience, for Mom's sake.

5.
THE FIRST REUNION

It was a cold but special Saturday morning on the 28th of November, 1998. I was to meet Maureen for the first time. I would come face to face with the sister my parents had given away for adoption. The tension was unbearable. Neither of us had seen pictures of the other so we did not know what to expect.

Reservations were for 6:30 p.m. Gord and I wanted to get there early to ensure everything was perfect. It took me forever to get ready and choose an outfit. Normally it takes me very little time; my hair is curly and long so there's no styling involved, and I don't wear much make-up. However, I wanted to look casually made-up and this took more effort than usual, mostly due to my nerves taking over.

On our drive to the restaurant, I cried. I was an emotional wreck and couldn't imagine what Maureen must have been feeling. I had spoken to Maureen briefly that morning just to confirm that she hadn't changed her mind, and she expressed how she felt nervous but couldn't wait to meet me. When Gord and I arrived at the restaurant I spoke with Nick, the owner, regarding what was about to transpire. He was honored that we had chosen his establishment to experience this life altering moment. It was only 6 p.m., and I found myself wishing that we hadn't arrived so early. We were at our table just sitting and waiting for my new sister to walk through the entrance with her husband. The hostess of the restaurant was made aware of the circumstances, and she came over to our table to congratulate me. The hostess was misty-eyed at the mere thought of what was about to happen, which of course set me off. I was trembling and crying, so Gord ordered some wine in the hopes of calming my nerves. Gord and I talked, and he tried his best to relax me, but admitted that he was nervous for me. How many times in life, would one experience a moment like this?

Time marched on and still, no one who fitted Maureen's description came through the door. It was now 6:30 and with the arrival of each new face, my heart would skip a beat. The restaurant was filling up. Every customer was sitting down to be served but no one resembled my sister, or fitted the image of what I thought my sister should look like. I began to think that my sister would never arrive; perhaps she'd had a change of heart and had decided not to come after all. I could not bear that thought, so I tried to put it out of my mind immediately. It is the traffic, I told myself. It is nerves, but she *is* coming.

Finally, a couple walked in and started walking towards our table. This girl didn't look like me at all, so I was confused as to whether they were heading towards our table or not. But I stood up just in case, and as the girl drew closer, she asked, "Debbie?" and I answered with, "Maureen." Initially, we just looked at one another, but then I made my way to her and I gave her a big hug. Oddly enough, we didn't cry as I anticipated we would. We introduced our husbands to one another and sat down. Maureen sat facing me and we kept smiling at one another. She apologized for being late and explained that they had in fact arrived on time, but that she had been sitting in their vehicle trying to get the courage to go through with it.

We were all talking; our husbands talking to each other as Maureen and I chatted about our lives. As she spoke, I couldn't help but stare. I stared at her smile, her laugh, her sparkly eyes, but most of all at her hands; the way she held them was so much like Mom. I didn't recognize the resemblance at first, but Maureen was like Mom in so many ways. I hadn't seen these characteristics in six years, and it felt a little spooky and wonderful at the same time. As Maureen spoke, I didn't really hear her words as the only thing I could concentrate on was the feeling of complete joy in my heart. Maureen managed to bring back memories of the mother I missed dearly, and it suddenly occurred to me that this woman, sitting across from me, was most definitely her "mother's daughter."

Suddenly, I heard my name being called. I looked at Maureen, and she said that I was staring at her. I felt so embarrassed and apologized. I then explained why it seemed like I left this world for a few minutes. In fact, I did better than that; I took the photographs of my parents out of my wallet to show Maureen. One was a black and white picture of them in their early twenties. When Maureen looked at it, she gasped, looked up at me, and said that she looked just like her. I could see the relief in Maureen's face as she said she was wondering who she looked like since we didn't look alike. She realized, as I did, when we first saw one another that we did not look like sisters. I think we were both a little disappointed at that. But I was so happy to see just how much she resembled Mom. None of us siblings looked much like Mom, with perhaps the exception of Lenny; but even he didn't resemble Mom nearly so much as Maureen did. It actually felt a little scary, but at the same time, very rewarding. I remembered details about Mom that I had not thought of in years. Maureen's mannerisms were also very similar to Mom's and I told her as much. She had a tear in her eye as I spoke of "our" mother. Maureen had wanted so desperately to meet her birth mother and now, all she had were pictures and my memories.

We ate dinner and spoke incessantly about our lives. Maureen showed me a picture of her daughter, Megan, who was so beautiful. It felt good having another young niece in the family. After we finished eating, Gord suggested something that I did not expect; he suggested we all go over to Tina's house so that we could get the two meetings done on the same night. Maureen's husband, Paul, said it was a great idea, but when Maureen looked at me, I could see that she was a little scared and apprehensive. It was enough meeting one long lost sister in a night, but two? I told her that Tina would love to see her, but that it was her decision. I guess the few drinks Maureen had over dinner had relaxed her considerably because she agreed to meet Tina.

I called Tina on my cellular phone. I told her that I had a surprise for her and that we would be at her house in twenty minutes. Tina knew me well and said, "She's coming here now?" I had to say yes, and her first response was that she didn't have any milk for coffee. I told her that she had a few minutes to go and pick up what she needed. Before hanging up I said, "Tina, be prepared. She's just like Mom."

We arrived at Tina's house and knocked on the door. Maureen and Paul stood behind Gord and I. Tina answered with teary eyes, and as soon as she saw Maureen, she ran and hugged her. They both had tears streaming down their faces. As I watched, I started crying. We three sisters began laughing at our emotional outburst. Maureen told Tina that even she and I hadn't cried. Tina was surprised since I was the emotional cripple in the family. Tina looked Maureen over with a smile, turned to me and said, "Yes, she is just like Mom, except the nose." I had already told Maureen that I wasn't sure whose nose she had inherited, but it was similar to the nose of our youngest brother Rocky.

After an hour or so Maureen really didn't feel well and apologetically said that she had to leave. We felt sorry for her, as well as disappointment that the night had come to an end. As we hugged goodbye, all I could think of was what a trooper Maureen was. She had the guts to meet not only one, but two of her birth sisters on the same day. And that, to me, was unbelievable. No wonder she didn't feel well!

After she left, Tina and I both agreed that it was as if Mom had just left the room. The resemblance was eerie and one that struck us both. Perhaps we take family resemblance for granted since we see each other everyday; perhaps we look at our siblings and parents without actually seeing them. When confronted with an almost exact copy, it suddenly hits you. I was struck by the sheer physical lineage of our family; the genetic threads that bound us all together. Her face, her voice and even her mannerisms screamed, Mom. It was obvious that, somehow, this fragile thing called a personality is an identity shared from person to person; mother to daughter, father to son. As the door closed to Tina's house, it was as if the spirit of Mom had visited us. It made me feel secure again, as if I could feel her arms around me or as if she was telling me the pain would go away.

The next morning, I called Memère Rose and gave her the details of the meeting with Maureen. She was pleased to be given a second opportunity to know her granddaughter. When I mentioned how much Maureen resembled Mom, I heard the line go silent. Memère Rose and Mom were as close as any mother and daughter could be; everyday, Memère Rose looked at the photo of Mom that I had given her. I knew she would be emotional at the thought that her second eldest grandchild was continuing the family resemblance.

I told her that I would bring Maureen and her daughter, Megan, to her house in the next couple of weeks. Excitedly, she said she would like that very much. She was looking forward to speaking with Maureen and explaining the reasons surrounding her adoption. I knew Memère Rose held a tremendous amount of guilt for the two adoptions, but she definitely had her reasons and valid explanations as far as I was concerned. Memère Rose was excited about finding both of her missing grandchildren, but I warned her that the chances of finding *both* were very slim indeed.

After I put the phone down, I called Lenny. He and Rocky were both made aware of the adopted babies just after the death of Mom. They didn't discuss it with me in detail and I wasn't sure if they had

THE FISRT REUNION

even believed what they had been told. At that time, Lenny had asked a few questions, but Rocky seemed to be in denial.

When Lenny was told of the previous night's events he did not seem concerned at all. He was pleased that it made Tina, Memère Rose and I happy, but he said that he had no interest in meeting Maureen at that time. I heard no malice in his voice, only that he was in a certain amount of disbelief about the entire situation, and so perhaps, it was not yet his time to become as excited as Tina and I.

My next call was to our youngest brother, Rocky, and his reaction took me totally by surprise. He first said that he didn't know what I was talking about and that he was never told about the adoptions. I said that I specifically remembered telling him after Mom's death. I figured he must have been in so much pain from her death that he had totally blocked it out of his mind. I felt very sorry for Rocky. He was only twenty years old when he lost his mother, who was also his best friend. Mom was everything to him. He was so terribly devastated by her death that he withdrew from everybody and everything.

I mentioned that Tina met our new sister as well, and how we both really liked her and thought she was the spitting image of Mom. Rocky went silent, and I felt bad that this news was so overwhelming for him. However, he did say that it was cool and would like to meet her some day in the near future. Rocky was more open-minded than I expected him to be, considering that he was only now, for the first time, acknowledging our sisters. Naturally, this pleased me.

I sat back in my swivel chair and wondered for a while about the different reactions I had received; especially the differences between the men and the women I had told. My brothers weren't the only men that had reacted strangely about our sisters; my male friends were equally weird about it. Many of them asked questions like, "How can you be sure they are your sisters? What are the exact details of the birth?" It was as if the whole idea of giving birth to a child made you more receptive to accepting new people and new experiences. I was completely open to my new sisters and so was Tina and Memère Rose, but my brothers' reactions had surprised me.

I decided to call Maureen and check that she was ok after the night before. She was thankful I called; she apologized once again for not feeling well and having to cut short her visit at Tina's house. I told her that I totally understood and that if I were in her shoes I would probably have felt the same, if not worse.

We spoke for about half an hour and she asked me who I had talked to about our meeting. I was pleased to let her in on my conversation with Memère Rose, who couldn't wait to meet her. I told her that our brothers were a little shocked and needed some time to deal with the reality. Maureen immediately defended Rocky and Lenny by saying that guys do not have the same emotions that women do, especially when it came to things like that. I agreed with her and said that it would just take longer for them to accept having another sister in their lives. I also said that I hoped she would be patient with them. She definitely seemed to understand and even made excuses for the brothers she had yet to meet.

Maureen briefly discussed her past and the reasons for the distance presently between herself and her parents. She spoke highly of her father but had nothing except resentment towards her mother. Maureen hadn't spoken with her brother, who was adopted four years prior to her, in at least ten years. She rarely spoke to her sister, whom her parents had conceived seven years after Maureen's adoption. I never asked Maureen what exactly transpired in her childhood to create such animosity towards her family since I didn't want her to relive the pain. I also felt it was very personal and thought that if she felt like telling me, then she would; maybe in time, she would see that I just wanted to help her. I offered my support, but I felt it was not my place to offer her guidance. I was her new family now and more importantly, her friend. I just hoped Maureen would find comfort and happiness in what the future held for us.

I could feel a connection growing between us; it was small at first and hardly noticeable, but as we talked, it became more and more obvious. It took a while to realize. But pretty soon I knew that it was because we cared about each other, and for the ready made family that we had become. Both of us, picked from nowhere, and given a new family with a new history, and a new way of thinking. We were not only adjusting to it; we were enjoying it and growing well, together.

The next family member Maureen would be meeting was Memère Rose, her grandmother. I became emotional just thinking about them reuniting. Memère Rose had met her once before; when Maureen was first born. And now, Memère Rose's dream of seeing this baby girl again one day would soon come true.

It was two weeks before Christmas and I was driving again. This time I was on my way to pick up Maureen and Megan, to take them to meet Memère Rose. I had rented a car since Gord and I both drove a two-seater. I could barely contain myself when I thought of the meeting that was about to happen. I was also excited about meeting my new niece Megan. I stopped the car just outside their house and waited for a moment to compose myself before walking slowly up the path to their front door.

A pretty baby girl with piercing blue eyes, and an obviously wise head on her shoulders greeted me at the door. We hugged and she gave me a huge smile that made me feel relaxed and welcome. Maureen came running down the stairs and we hugged as well; it truly felt like we had known each other for a while. At least, on my part, I felt no uneasiness. Maureen and I talked for a few minutes as she quickly showed me around her house. Then, we were on our way.

Memère Rose's house was a little over an hour's drive away, so there was time to talk to Maureen and Megan and to get to know them a little better. We had decided to stay overnight at Memère Rose's house. I hoped it wouldn't be too much for Maureen, but we discussed it and she seemed fine with the idea; she was not alone after all.

I rang the doorbell to my grandparent's huge ranch bungalow in Marmora while Maureen began getting Megan from the car seat. Memère Rose opened the door, and immediately, she and Maureen embraced for what seemed like minutes. They just held each other and whispered, "I love you." After all these years, these two women were meeting for the second time in their lives. The first time was an all too brief moment in a hospital maternity room. Memère Rose hugged little Megan and said that now she had two beautiful great granddaughters. To my surprise, Memère Rose thought Maureen only slightly resembled Mom and thought she looked more like Rocky, instead. However, I realized that when I first met Maureen, it took me a few minutes to see Mom in her.

Maureen, Memère Rose, and I sat and talked in the family room while Megan played with some of her toys and kept Leandre entertained. Memère Rose immediately started to explain the circumstances surrounding the two adoptions, and her reasons for not allowing Mom to keep Maureen. Earlier, Maureen had told me that it didn't matter, but at that moment I could see in her face that it did matter to her; she wished that she had been raised with the love and attention that my family gave.

Maureen is a very gentle, thoughtful person, and she didn't want to see her birth grandmother upset over something that occurred so many years ago and could never be changed. She told Memère Rose that it was okay and that she didn't need to explain herself any further.

Maureen was very interested in learning more about her birth mother. Memère Rose showed her photo albums that contained pictures of us as children, and of Mom from the time she was born, up until the time she passed away. The conversation about Mom made us all weep. Memère Rose couldn't help but cry while talking about Mom's last few months. Maureen became emotional as she witnessed the pain Memère Rose and I still felt at losing Mom.

Later, we all sat down for dinner in the kitchen and had a wonderful home cooked meal. Megan loved the ham, and we couldn't believe how much food that little girl could put in her belly. As we all sat chatting, I noticed Memère Rose staring at Maureen. I could tell that Memère Rose was now beginning to recognize the characteristics that Maureen had inherited from her birth mother. I didn't say anything, except, I asked Memère Rose to look at Maureen's hands; they looked identical to Mom's and even the way she held them was exactly the same. Memère Rose laughed and had to agree with me.

We went to bed pretty early as we were all emotionally drained by our experience. I couldn't help feeling that we were all becoming a little closer to each other. Even though the one truly important person was missing, in so many ways she was still there; not only in spirit, but also in the hearts, blood, and minds of the women that we were, and the woman that Megan would become. I began to feel as though this tiny group of women were the frame around Mom; we were her past, her present, and her future all contained within one room.

The next day, we all woke up very early as the sun streamed in through the windows. Maureen and I packed up by midday and we said our emotional goodbyes. Leandre had so much fun with Megan. He thought she was the cutest little girl. Memère Rose and Maureen hugged each other goodbye and I said my usual teary goodbyes to my grandparents.

After dropping off Maureen and Megan at their house, I drove home and wondered what it would be like when they met the rest of my family. It was at times like this, that I thanked God they were who they were; kind, loving, and honest. But it had been an excruciating time for every one of them, and it was taking its toll on the adhesion that held us together. I hoped that it would make us stronger and not pull us apart.

THE FISRT REUNION

Christmas was drawing closer and I wanted the entire family to be together on Christmas Eve; the traditional time for our family to come together. But I knew that it was a pipe dream as Aunt Linda was hosting the party, and she still wasn't ready to meet Maureen. Maybe Christmas was not the appropriate time for Aunt Linda to meet Maureen.

Maureen was thrilled that Tina and I were going to visit them for Christmas. I bought Maureen a little present; one I hoped she would cherish forever. Maureen opened the box and took out the Christmas ornament. Written on the front was "Sisters – 1998." She appeared to be on the verge of tears so I figured she liked it. I also gave her a framed, professional photograph of all her sisters and brothers. It was the same one we had made for Memère Rose's 75th birthday. It was an absolutely beautiful picture, and Maureen loved it as well. Maureen opened Tina's gift and apologized for not buying us anything in return, but both me and Tina agreed that another sister and niece were just about the best present anyone could ever get for Christmas.

The party at Aunt Linda's was extremely uncomfortable. Memère Rose and Leandre were both very upset that Maureen was not invited. However, as time passed the reason for this became apparent: Dad. Even though I thought it was a wonderful opportunity lost, deep in my heart, I knew that the reunion between a daughter and her birth father should be a private one.

It had certainly been a Christmas to remember, and I was looking forward to what the New Year would bring. I had decided that this would be a time of new beginnings; a time when we could remember without sadness and try to move on with our lives. It had been so trying these last few years, but things were really coming together, literally, you could say.

SISTERS REVEALED

6.
GETTING TO KNOW MAUREEN

It was early 1999. Gord and I met Maureen and Paul at a restaurant they had raved about, close to their house in Oshawa. They wanted to treat us to dinner and reciprocate our first meeting. Besides, it gave us a chance to bond further. It was a steak and seafood restaurant, and we had a fabulous time. I loved watching Maureen talk and most of all laugh. It brought back so many memories of Mom and it warmed my heart. We spent a good couple of hours eating, talking, laughing, and just getting further acquainted. It felt so right when I hugged Maureen goodbye. We didn't have a lot in common as far as hobbies and interests, but our personalities clicked, and she truly felt like a sister to me.

Every time we spoke, I felt as if I knew Maureen a little more. Soon, we stopped feeling and acting like sisters who had only just met and started instead, to relax in each other's company. It allowed the conversations to just drift wherever they needed to go; it felt just like we were old friends chatting over coffee about everything and nothing.

March was fast approaching. It was Lenny's 30th birthday on the 14th. Our family rarely celebrated birthdays together, but being such an important age we decided to get together and share it with him. Tina and I thought it would be a good idea to ask Lenny if he was ready to meet Maureen and if he would like to see her and Paul at his birthday dinner. I called him, fully expecting to hear more reasons why he wasn't ready or willing to meet Maureen. But to my surprise he agreed. I truly thought I had misheard him, and there was a long silence between us before I was able to respond. I told him how excited I was, but that he could take some time to really think about it since it was his big day. I didn't want him to be stressed out on his birthday. Lenny said that he would be all right and that he would meet her at the restaurant. It dawned on me that Rocky was going to be there as well and I asked Lenny what he thought Rocky would say about it. Lenny didn't think Rocky would mind, but suggested I talk to him.

So I called Rocky and told him the plans and he just said, "Cool." That was it. There was going to be no more trouble, no more periods of anxiety, no more waiting; my brothers were going to meet my sister at last. I could not contain myself thinking how great it would be when, finally, everyone could be together as one big family - a family that was getting bigger all the time.

We made reservations at a local restaurant that was just a few minutes away from both Maureen and Lenny. I telephoned Maureen to tell her the news. She was astonished and nearly in tears. Then questions started raining down the phone line, "What was she going to wear? Did they really want to meet her? Did I force them?" I jokingly reassured her that they were ready to meet their "big, bad sister" and she laughed.

It was Saturday, the day before Lenny's birthday party. I called Maureen and she confessed how nervous she was about meeting her brothers. I didn't blame her. Between the last few months of waiting and our brothers' unsure feelings about meeting her, I could only imagine the fear in Maureen's mind. She had been nervous about meeting Tina and myself, but we had both expressed our desire to meet her, which made Maureen feel welcome. Moreover, I had spoken with Maureen over the phone before we had met. She didn't have any communication at all with our brothers, so she didn't know what to expect. I assured Maureen that they were friendly guys and that Tina and I would be present to help ease any tension. I forewarned her that Rocky tended to be very quiet and not to misread his lack of conversation as anything negative. We confirmed the time and place and said we'd see each other tomorrow.

I admitted to Gord how nervous I was about Lenny's birthday dinner. I knew my brothers were nice, but I just hoped they would make Maureen feel welcomed into our family, like Tina and I had done. Once in bed, I prayed that the next day would be a success.

Gord and I arrived at the restaurant almost half an hour early. We wanted to ensure that if Paul and Maureen were early, they wouldn't be sitting alone. This was Lenny's big 30th birthday, but it seemed almost insignificant compared to what was about to happen. Tina and Rocky arrived together ten minutes after Gord and I. The four of us were sitting at the bar having a drink, trying to calm our nerves, before Maureen and Paul arrived. The waitress sat us at our table, and we made small talk while we anxiously waited. Rocky seemed as calm as a cucumber, but I knew he was nervous.

Twenty minutes or so after arriving, Lenny hurried in and quickly sat down at the table. We wished him "Happy Birthday." While I was hugging him, I noticed Paul and Maureen at the doorway. Lenny said that he had just walked in with them and knew who she was but didn't want to say anything. He admitted that he already saw the resemblance to Mom. I don't know about the others, but as Maureen and Paul were walking towards our table, my stomach performed cartwheels, and my heart quickened its pace.

When they reached the table, both Tina and I gave Maureen a big calming hug. Then, we made the introductions to Lenny and Rocky, and they both hugged her. There were tears in my eyes as I witnessed them hugging, but they all seemed so calm. Maureen recognized which brother was which from the pictures she had seen of them and immediately she commented on how she and Lenny looked a little alike. Maureen also admitted to recognizing Lenny when they were walking into the restaurant, but like Lenny, she didn't want to say anything.

For the first hour, we just drank beer and talked. There was no lack of conversation as we all took turns speaking, including Rocky and Lenny. They told her about their lives and about their memories of Mom. Maureen spoke about her feelings at suddenly being presented with a ready made family after all these years. I could tell she was a little nervous being the centre of attention, but that was how we wanted it to be. She was the guest of honor, despite it being Lenny's birthday.

It still made me sad that Maureen had never gotten to meet her birth mother. She was, after all, the person that she wanted to meet the most. I was determined, however, to make up for this and to make Maureen's time with us as happy as I could.

We ate dinner, talked and drank, and there didn't seem to be any tension in the air. Everyone was having a wonderful time. After we finished eating, Lenny opened his presents. Then, we ate some cake. Being Sunday night, we couldn't stay too late or drink too much, so we left at around 9 p.m. The few hours we shared together were fabulous. As I sat looking around at my family, I silently wept while I imagined Mom up above, looking down on all of us and being so happy that we found Maureen. It was unfortunate that Dad wasn't present. Maureen told me however, from the very beginning, that she was happy meeting her sisters, and that if she met her brothers or her father, it would be a bonus. The glow on Maureen's face after meeting her brothers spoke for itself; Maureen was obviously in very high spirits. Maybe one day, in the near future, she would meet her birth father.

We all left at the same time. Lenny thanked us for the dinner and presents as we said our goodbyes. I told Maureen that I would call her soon. As we hugged she whispered in my ear that she thought her new found brothers were great and that she just loved them.

Over the next few days, I called Lenny and Rocky and thanked them for their willingness to let Maureen into their lives. They thought she was really sweet. As it turned out, Rocky and Maureen had similar hobbies, and they got on the best of all. I had expected the brother/sister relationship to take awhile to develop since they were men, and they treated these situations differently to women. Lina, the Children's Aid Counselor, had warned me about this. Apparently, it is mostly women who are involved in searches and reunions. In my own experience, I felt as if women were more inclined to building relationships than men.

I called Maureen to get her feedback on the night and heard much the same thing. She mentioned her connection with Rocky and said that overall, the evening had been a great success. I was so glad to hear this from her. As the person responsible for bringing everyone together, I felt almost like the mother hen clucking over my chicks. It was always good to hear that everyone was happy with how things were going. We talked a little about our eldest sister, Mom and Dad's firstborn, but I said it was almost hopeless to try and find her. She would have to register with the agency, and because she was the oldest, this seemed unlikely now. Maureen agreed, but we both said that we wouldn't give up hope.

We also spoke about the next event that would bring our family together. Maureen mentioned her daughter Megan's second birthday on April 3rd. She was having a small birthday party at her house, and she wanted all of us to attend and hopefully meet Paul's mother and sister as well. Apparently, they had been very supportive to Maureen during her search and the meeting of her birth family. Maureen sounded so excited about having a family gathering, and an actual family that would take part in her life. Up until now, Megan's birthday and other holidays included Paul's family only, since Maureen's family was never present.

Maureen and I spoke every week during the time leading up to Megan's birthday; we wanted everything to be just right for her little girl, who had also faced so many strange and different changes in her life.

The 3rd of April approached quickly and Megan turned two years old. Tina's daughter, Shanelle, was so excited about meeting her little cousin and aunt for the first time. She was only six, so I don't think she fully understood the adoption stuff. She didn't question who they were; she was just excited that she now had a cousin. Everybody showed up except Lenny who had told Rocky that he wasn't feeling well. We met Paul's family and they were really nice people. I could see that his mother was quite emotional regarding Maureen's experience. It was obvious that she was thrilled to see Maureen so happy with a family that welcomed her into their hearts. Megan and Shanelle really hit it off as they played with the other kids. Shanelle was like a big sister to her. Megan opened all her presents, or should I say, ripped them open. She seemed to like everything. She was so cute with her big curls.

I told Paul's family that Megan's birth date was also the date of my parents' wedding anniversary. I thought it was just me who had these spiritual feelings and believed in destiny and fate, but it appeared that Maureen shared my beliefs too, up to a point. Gord felt I was a little wacky at times but he didn't ridicule me. It was a fun birthday party and once again, Maureen and I bonded further. Every event seemed to bring us closer.

Over the next few weeks and months, Maureen gradually became a firm member of our family. Looking back, it did not take long; probably a reflection on the genetic threads that bound us together. Time was traveling so fast, but we felt as if we had known her for years already. Of course, sometimes I felt as though I was being a little overbearing, I desperately wanted her to join in, to feel comfortable, and to feel as though she belonged.

April soon turned into the long hot holiday months of summer. Everyone was taking vacations. Maureen and I were still speaking regularly but had not seen each other for a while, so we decided we would have a mini break together. I suggested she come and stay the weekend with Gord and me, without Paul or Megan. It had been a while since she had been away from her family, and she jumped at the chance.

So, in July, I drove round to Maureen's house. She was coming over for a sleepover! This was, of course, Maureen's first visit to my house, and she commented on how nice everything looked, and how inviting it was. We sat and looked at photograph albums for a while before we decided to go out for dinner. We had a blast that first night, and stayed up very late, talking. With the few too many drinks we had consumed we seemed to loosen up, and we began talking about some silly things and also some serious issues. We went from laughing to crying. We were emotionally spent by the time we turned in at 2 a.m. It was a remarkable feeling to have my new sister in my house sleeping only a couple of doors away from me.

I closed my eyes and imagined what it might have been like to have two more older sisters in the house when we were children. Then it struck me that things would have been completely different. My parents might not have had me at all, or my bothers. The family would have been remarkably different, and not at all the family that I knew. It was hard not to think, then, that everything happens for a purpose. Mom's illness had prompted the search for my two sisters, and their adoptions had made my family what it was.

I felt as though there were hands guiding me along the way, but these hands were not the hands of God; they were the hands of Mom, looking after us all as she had always done in life.

We awoke the next morning with mild hangovers, but it was nothing a good breakfast couldn't cure. It was a beautiful sunny day, and we took in the sun while sitting on my deck for a couple of hours. Maureen had her hair up again, and she reminded me so much of Mom. We lounged around all day, and I went through my wardrobe to see if there was anything Maureen wanted that I didn't wear anymore. There were only a few shirts that were suitable, but luckily we wore the same size shoe, so I gave her a couple of pairs. I also gave her a pair of gold earrings that I inherited from Mom. I really wanted Maureen to have something special that belonged to her birth mother. She hugged and thanked me.

That night we met with Tina, her sister-in-law, Pam, and Pam's husband, Dave for dinner. We were also going to meet Tina's new boyfriend, Steve, who none of us had met yet. We went to a local Italian restaurant in my hometown of Aurora and had a wonderful dinner. We had just finished when an attractive guy walked in and came straight to our table. It was Tina's boyfriend, Steve, and he was introduced to all of us. It felt strange calling him Steve since Tina's ex-husband's name was Steve as well. He seemed a little nervous and cracked a few jokes.

Gord and I invited everyone back to our house and they accepted. We took advantage of the gorgeous summer night, and sat outside on the deck, talking over a couple of drinks. I think Maureen felt good that this time she wasn't alone in meeting someone for the first time; we all had just met Steve and were trying to get acquainted. It was an interesting night, and I was so pleased that Maureen was having a good weekend.

The next day we slept in a little. After breakfast, Maureen and I did a little shopping. I drove her home in the late afternoon and stepped in to get a quick hug from Megan.

On my drive home, I reflected on my weekend with Maureen and felt fortunate to have her in my life. I was also thinking about children for some reason. Gord and I almost never spoke about children since he had decided, at thirty, that he never wanted any and had a vasectomy. I agreed when we married that children were not in my future, but I guess all this recent family stuff made me feel maternal. I was thinking a child was something I now wanted in our lives. There comes a point in everyone's life when you realize your own mortality. You look around and wonder what you will leave to the world – things, words, books?

When I arrived home, I gathered the courage to discuss my feelings with Gord about wanting a child. I truly expected him to turn a deaf ear to this much dreaded topic but he agreed instead. I almost fell off my chair from complete shock and excitement. We knew we couldn't conceive the conventional way, so we decided to make an appointment with our family doctor to discuss our options.

I saw my family doctor the following week, and he recommended a fertility doctor. I called, and the waiting list was three months long. I was a little disappointed but made an appointment for late September. What were a few extra months when we had been married for eleven years and had only just now decided to have a child.

I told my family about our plans, and they were all ecstatic; especially Maureen who thought Gord and I would make great parents. We had no idea what our options were, but we didn't care if we had to use a donor. In fact, Gord even suggested we adopt. The thought seemed interesting and intriguing especially given the history of my family, and the revelations that I had been experiencing in the last few months. I felt as though it would be my chance to give something back for the wonderful gift of my new sister. However, at this early stage I really wanted to be pregnant and hopefully have a child of our own first.

The next few months flew by as Maureen and I continued to get closer. It truly felt like she had been my sister for years. Gord and I had our appointment at the fertility clinic, and we left the clinic very happy. There was a way we could have our own child without Gord having a vasectomy reversal. The highest success rate for pregnancy was in-vitro fertilization but at this point, the doctor thought I should just try artificial insemination. None of the women in my family had problems conceiving. I was very healthy, so we were going to try the least complicated method first. We felt as though things were moving in the right direction, not only did I have a new sister, but I might even have a child of my own to add to the family.

We decided to book a vacation for our eleventh wedding anniversary. We agreed on a three night stay in the Bahamas at an all-inclusive resort. It was quite expensive, but we needed to get away before starting the baby making process. We arrived in the Bahamas on the 10th of November, and our anniversary was on the 12th of November. We had horrible rainy weather, and we experienced quite a few problems with the hotel. They were overbooked, and the lineups for the fine dining restaurants were outrageous. The actual night of our anniversary was a total disaster to say the least. I cried because I was so frustrated. By our departure day on Sunday, things seemed to be better; unfortunately, it was a little too late.

Gord checked our voicemail messages at home and the office before we left the hotel. He came to the poolside to inform me that there was a message from Lina on Friday, asking me to call her first thing on Monday morning. My initial reaction was that she was calling for a follow-up report on my relationship with Maureen since it had been almost exactly one year since we met one another. It seemed logical that Lina would be curious to see how things were going and possibly close the file.

I thought of all the things I had to say to her about Maureen, and how grateful I was to the Society for giving me the chance to meet her. It was good to hear from her while out here in the Bahamas; it reminded me of all the good things I had at home to go back to. On the plane ride home, I kept thinking about the message. If it was just a follow-up call then why did she ask me to call her first thing Monday morning? Why didn't she say it was a follow up call? Are these things routine in an organization like the CCAS? I talked it over with Gord, and he agreed with me that it was probably a mere formality. I settled back in my seat, looked out the window, and noticed how small the world was.

I had trouble sleeping the night we returned home from our vacation. I had to start my first attempt at getting pregnant as well as return Lina's call the next day. I had to wake up at 5:30 a.m. since cycle monitoring was done extremely early. I told Gord that I would call Lina once I arrived at the office. Gord and I still worked together, so he would be present in case I needed his support when I called CCAS.

I arrived at the office at 9:30 a.m. and filled Gord in on the procedures I had endured at the clinic. I had so much on my mind that I could barely remember what I had gone through, but I excitedly told him what they had told me, and we discussed our chances of success. I was desperate to phone Lina and find out her news, so I picked up the phone and dialed her number. After a few rings, I got her voicemail. I left a message for her to contact me at work and went about sorting out the many things I had to do on one of the busiest days I could remember.

At about 11:30 a.m., my phone rang. I took a deep breath and answered on the second ring. Lina was on the other end of the line, and she began the conversation by asking me if I was seated. I said I was. Lina then proceeded to tell me that there was another match at the adoption registry; my eldest sister had registered a couple of months ago. I didn't cry this time since I had imagined her telling me this, but I was definitely in shock. There was a long silence between us, and she asked me if I was all right. I lied and said that I was fine.

Before Lina could tell me anymore, I blurted out that I wanted to wait a couple of weeks before dealing with it. She responded by saying she understood my reluctance since my situation with Maureen had caused me months of anguish in the beginning stages. She assured me that this time things would be different. At this point in our conversation, I hadn't asked Lina any questions. I assumed Lina was calling me first to see if I was still interested and would then try to contact this sister. But I was totally wrong. Lina asked me to hear her out and that she had great news. Firstly, she told me that she had already spoken to my sister to see if she was still interested in finding her birth family and more importantly, to advise her that her birth mother was deceased. Lina referred to my sister as Patricia, and I asked her if this was my sister's real name or if it was the name that Mom had given her. Lina explained that because she had already spoken to my sister, the procedures would be very different this time around. She said that Patricia was her real name but most people called her Trish.

I was filled with excitement and wanted to hear more. Lina told me that Trish lived in London with her husband and two daughters. I started with excitement; London was only about a two hour drive away from us. I could go and see her almost immediately. Lina laughed and said, "Not London, Ontario. London, England."

I didn't think I'd heard her properly, so I made her repeat herself. How on earth, did my sister end up in a country so far away? Lina then told me how Trish's parents adopted her in Toronto, and then they moved to New York City when Trish was two. When Trish turned eleven, her parents decided to move back to their homeland of Ireland. As Lina spoke, I was trying to make sense of this news and remembered what I had read in the non-identifying information that I had received. Her parents were both in the medical field; presumably, it was their careers that forced them to move to New York. It was probably their life ambition to move back to Ireland to be with their family and friends.

Lina told me that after Trish received her Ph.D., at the age of twenty-five, she had found a job in England and had lived there ever since. I asked if my sister was a doctor. Lina said that Trish was not in medicine, but chemistry; she worked for a chemical company. I was already so proud to have such a smart sister, but I have to admit I felt somewhat jealous. I didn't even have a post graduate degree, and now my new sister was referred to as "Doctor". Lina then advised me that Trish's husband was a scientist and that they had met at the company they both still work at. They have two daughters; a four year old and a seventeen month old baby girl. I was thrilled to hear that I had gained two more nieces.

I confessed to Lina that I felt overwhelmed by all this information. She explained that Trish felt the same, but was also excited to hear that she had a whole new family in Canada, and couldn't wait to speak with me. She also informed me that Trish was willing to forego the usual procedures, of letter writing and photographs, which meant that we would be able to move faster, providing I was in full agreement.

Things were moving so fast; it all seemed to close in. For years now, I had dreamt of the moment when everything would come together: my two sisters and, perhaps, my own baby but now that the moment was finally here, I was at a loss at what to do. I wanted to take stock of the situation and have a little time to work through everything that was going on.

I truly was excited about the prospect of talking to Trish, but at the same time, I was overwhelmed with my present life. I told Lina that I wanted to wait a couple of weeks. I just couldn't give Trish the undivided attention I felt she deserved with the pregnancy issue hanging over me. Lina empathized with my situation and said she would convey my feelings to Trish.

I told Lina how difficult it was to believe that all this was happening; that I was to meet both of my sisters. She agreed that this was a huge coincidence. Lina then said the words that I felt silly and uneasy to say out loud, "Your mother has been working overtime in heaven."

My hand ached from gripping the phone so tightly. I felt hot and flustered. I looked over to Gord, and he came to my desk and hugged me. I held him tightly and cried on his shoulder. The unimaginable had just happened; a dream that I never truly believed would come true had just been realized. But why now? I had so much going on in my life at this moment. I was working on making another dream come true; my dream of having a baby. I expressed my concerns to Gord about feeling selfish. There was a woman in England who was so excited about speaking with me that she was willing to cut through the red tape, and here I was asking her to wait a couple of weeks.

Gord agreed that I was being a little selfish, but he said that I had a right to my own feelings. If I wasn't ready, then maybe it would be better to wait. As he spoke, it dawned on me that I was punishing my new sister because of the unpleasant experience of waiting I had with Maureen. It didn't seem fair when I put myself in Trish's shoes. Lina told me that she was an only child and that her parents hadn't adopted any more children. Trish was now willing to open herself up to a completely new family; she was going from an only child with no known siblings, to having three sisters and two brothers. How on earth, could I make her wait? Gord and I both agreed that I should sleep on this dilemma and call Lina the next day.

I was desperate to call Tina and share with her the good news, but Gord suggested we have lunch so I could try to relax a bit before another emotional phone call. I think he wanted me to float back down to earth. He knew I wasn't thinking clearly and I was still in a state of shock. We went to lunch but I didn't eat much. We spoke about all the information Lina had provided me about my new sister. I smiled so much that my face hurt; I knew in my heart what I would do from here.

I called Tina right after lunch. I started the conversation the same way Lina had with me by asking if Tina was seated. However, before I could even say anything, she had guessed why I was phoning. Sometimes, in moments of clarity, you can put these second-guesses down to the tone of the voice or subtle cues in expression, but it is difficult not to think that there is another deeper level at work here. It's something connected to the collective unconscious that families share; the bond that ties them together and allows them to communicate over wide distances. We were both so emotional that it was hard to say anything. Again, I had tears streaming down my cheeks since not only was this a dream come true for me, but one for Tina as well. I finally pulled myself together and filled Tina in on everything I had learned from Lina about Trish. She was as impressed as I was about Trish having a doctorate. After speaking for a bit, I told her that I was contacting Lina tomorrow to get more information. I also told Tina that I would call Maureen that night to fill her in on the miraculous news.

I usually went to the gym to work out, but I was far too emotionally drained. I was absolutely exhausted. I had a long hot bath and while I was soaking, I remembered that Maureen worked nights. I would have to call her in the morning. I then started reminiscing about Maureen and how long it took to finally have telephone contact with her. I didn't want to complain, and it was well worth the wait when I heard her sweet voice for the first time, but I couldn't help but compare the different set of circumstances. This time, there was the possibility of hearing my eldest sister's voice on the phone as early as tomorrow; it was almost too quick!

I did not want Maureen to feel jealous or that someone else was taking her place. I had only known her a short while, but in that time I had grown to love her as a sister. She seemed too delicate and fragile at times and I did not want anything to come between us. On the other hand, she had a right to know about her eldest sister and to be placed in the picture as soon as possible. I stayed in the bath thinking it over for a little too long; leaving my fingers and toes puckered, but my head feeling better. I hoped that it would relax me enough to get some sleep that night.

I was walking past my spare bedroom soon after I awoke the next morning, and I caught a glimpse of the picture of Mom on the vanity.

I walked into the room and held the picture to my chest. I hugged it as if it was Mom in the flesh, and I thanked her for finding my other sister and bringing her to us. I truly felt like she had a hand in this miraculous search. She would have wanted us to meet one another and make our family complete.

I knew there were still surprises to come and that I had not reached the end of this amazing journey. I felt that, wherever it led, Mom was guiding us and looking out for us. If I closed my eyes, I could hear her soothing words and feel her near me again; encouraging me when I thought I could not go on and giving me strength when I felt weak and afraid. I desperately wanted to speak with her again, to tell her how much I missed her. But I also knew that none of this would have happened if it were not for her passing. We were all merely a part of her big plan, and I smiled to think of her pulling the strings to get us together again. Even though I wasn't sure if I was doing the right thing, I thought that I had to get in touch with Trish as soon as possible.

I left the house very early again for my cycle monitoring and reached the office at 8:30 a.m. I waited until Gord arrived before calling Lina to get an update and to let her know my feelings. Thankfully, she was at her desk when I called. She indicated that she had spoken with my new sister. Trish had understood my feelings about wanting to wait a couple of weeks to speak with her. Lina gave me Trish's phone number and said that Trish was waiting for my call; whether it was right away or in a couple of weeks after finding out my pregnancy results.

Lina and I spoke further about Trish. She gave me a description of her, and I was taken aback when she said that Trish had straight, light brown hair. Only Dad and Lenny had straight hair; all the girls had curly, dark brown hair. Then Lina began reading from what I gathered were the actual adoption papers, she noted that Mom named Trish "Rose Lisa". That did not surprise me since Memère's first name is Rose. It was apparent that Mom liked the name Lisa since she had also named Maureen, "Lisa Marie."

I then asked what Trish's full name was, and she said, Patricia Maureen. My heart skipped a beat, and I almost fell off my chair. Lina asked me what was wrong because of the long pause. I composed myself for a second and explained that not only did Mom give Trish and Maureen the same name of Lisa, but that Trish's adoptive parents had given Trish the same middle name as her sister! The girls had a common name given by Mom at birth, and continued to have a common name, albeit a different one, after adoption.

Again, I was aware of the almost spiritual connections that existed between my family members. Two girls who never even knew the other existed had been christened with the same name. The chances were astronomical and made me all the more convinced that the fate of my family was moving in the right direction. I knew, somehow, that I was in the right place doing the right things because everything added up.

Lina and I talked a little more about the name revelation and the difference between Maureen and Trish. Maureen had been so upset by the news of her birth mother's passing that she had unknowingly stalled her meeting with her siblings; meanwhile, Trish didn't dwell on the news of her birth mother and couldn't wait to meet her siblings. The entire experience of initially contacting Maureen had left me so nervous about meeting Trish; however, this time everything was already moving so quickly.

After speaking with Lina, I realized that I was punishing Trish for the worry and anxiety I had felt when I was waiting for Maureen. I decided that I was being selfish and that it was unfair of me to make her wait for weeks until I thought I was absolutely ready. How could I possibly make her wait?

It was too early to call her since she would just be getting home from work. Lina had mentioned to me that the best time to call her would be around 8:00 p.m. England time, which was 3:00 p.m. my time. This way, Trish's girls would be sleeping and she could give me her undivided attention. Gord and I went for lunch, but my nervousness chased away my appetite. In just a couple of hours, I would be speaking with my parents' firstborn child, and the sister I never imagined I would find.

I tried to get on with my day, but it was virtually impossible. I had so many things going around in my head, so many questions. How was Maureen going to feel about gaining another sister? How were Lenny and Rocky going to feel, especially so soon after getting to know Maureen? Was I going to be able to cope, going through it all again? I searched for some meaning in all of this and came up with the idea that this is how things should be; it is how my life was being guided.

7.
TRISH

At precisely 3:00 p.m., I dialed the number Lina gave me without realizing that it was a direct number. It sounds naïve, but I had never made an overseas call before and didn't know what to expect. I actually thought I would hear an operator's voice, who would then ask me who I wanted to be connected to.

Someone answered. I said, "Hello?" and asked for Trish since the person who answered had a really deep voice. I didn't think it was Trish's, but the person said, "Speaking." I was caught off guard since all the females in our family, with perhaps the exception of me, had high-pitched voices. All I could say was, "It's Debbie." The voice on the other end shrieked with excitement and suddenly, changed to a higher octave. I immediately told her how sorry I was for wanting to wait a couple of weeks before calling her and how foolish an idea it was since I was far too excited. She said that apologies weren't necessary and that she fully understood my position, but was concerned to hear that I had pregnancy issues. I didn't really want to talk about pregnancies with her at that point since it was our first conversation, but it certainly was an ice breaker. I told Trish how completely and utterly shocked I was to hear that my other sister had registered. I explained how odd it was that the two matches were almost exactly a year apart.

I quizzed Trish about her career and about how she ended up in England. She told me everything that Lina had said but in more detail. I felt very embarrassed since I had to ask Trish to repeat herself a few times, and it wasn't because of a bad phone connection. Her accent was quite heavy, which Lina had warned me about, but I wasn't prepared for what I assumed was a half Irish and half English accent. Trish was very funny with some of her Irish sayings, and she could already make me laugh.

She asked about Maureen, Tina, Lenny and Rocky, and I gave her a brief background on their lives. Then came the dreaded questions about Dad and she commented on how she couldn't believe that her birth parents ended up married and having all these other children. I realized that my parents' marriage must have been a shocking revelation for both Trish and Maureen. It's my perception that most adoptees think their mother couldn't afford to keep their children, or that their irresponsible father had not been willing to marry their young mother. I gave Trish a little bit of information about my parents' situation. Thinking it was a sore spot, I didn't want to go into great detail right away, but she didn't seem to care that much about the circumstances surrounding the adoptions. Trish admitted to having a great life and that she held no resentments.

Trish then explained something I had been wondering about; what made her decide to search for her birth family after all these years. She said that her mother had passed away two years ago. She hadn't wanted to search while her mother was alive since she didn't want to hurt her in any way. I told her that I was sorry to hear of her mother's passing and that I was able to relate to the painful experience of losing a mother. Just as I said that, I realized that Trish had actually lost two mothers even though she would only ever know one. It was obvious by the way Trish spoke of her parents that she loved them very much and had a great life with them. It was no wonder that she wasn't devastated like Maureen was when she found out about her birth mother's death. Everything was beginning to make sense to me.

Trish then spoke about how overwhelmed she was to find out about all her birth siblings. She explained how Lina didn't let her know about all of them in one phone call. Apparently, Lina didn't want to disclose everything to Trish at once. Trish found it frustrating since every time she spoke with Lina she didn't know what else would be revealed. She wondered exactly how many siblings she had and told Lina after her second conversation that she wanted to know everything and not to hold back any longer. When Trish spoke, she reminded me of myself.

I realized how different the phone call with Trish was, to that with Maureen. With Maureen, I felt like the elder sister. I felt as if it were me that needed to be reassuring and steadfast. With Trish, it was the opposite; I could feel myself shaking slightly and the tone in my voice altered. Perhaps it was Trish's accent, perhaps it was the surety in her voice, but the two conversations were completely different.

We spoke about the deaths of our mothers and the circumstances around them. I realized that Trish was an emotional person like the rest of us. It was evident that she missed her mother terribly, and she knew that I missed Mom just the same. Her feelings mirrored mine as she spoke of her mother. I was sure that Trish was a warm and loving daughter.

I don't know why, but I was constantly comparing myself to Trish during our conversation. Now it was time to ask the personal questions about her appearance. She described herself, including her height and weight. My first thoughts were that she had a tall, thin figure similar to Tina. Trish said that she was disappointed not to have curly hair like the rest of us girls, but I told her that we always want what we don't have and that I had wanted straight hair. We laughed as we spoke and it hit me that I was speaking with a sister who lived miles away and had a foreign accent. I couldn't believe how quickly all this happened!

We now had to address the problem of distance. Actually, the time difference was the biggest issue. Not so much for me, since I didn't work full time, but for Tina and Maureen who would have to speak to Trish on the weekends since they both worked full time. Trish asked me for Tina's and Maureen's phone numbers. I was glad she didn't ask for my brothers' numbers since this was going to be another hurdle to jump; or would it be different this time? I wasn't really sure, as this situation with Trish had already been so different from the situation with Maureen. I told Trish that it would be okay to call Tina and Maureen and that they would be absolutely thrilled to hear her voice. Then it dawned on me that I hadn't had a chance to speak with Maureen yet, let alone tell her that our other sister had been found. I asked Trish to wait a couple of days to contact Maureen, and I explained why.

Trish and I then spoke about when and where we were going to meet. Trish expressed her interest in coming to Canada, which made perfect sense considering that we were all here in Canada. My mind wandered to Memère Rose as Trish spoke of coming here. I shared my thoughts with Trish about how I felt Memère Rose would be delighted to finally meet the granddaughter who would make our family complete. My heart started racing as I spoke of Memère Rose. I couldn't wait to call her and let her know that her dream was being realized.

I knew that Memère Rose especially wanted to see Trish because she was Mom's firstborn. Somehow, even if you love all your kids the same, there is still something special about the first child. I knew that it would feel as though a circle had been completed; the missing piece slotted into place. It delighted me that Trish was so happy as well and that she seemed so comfortable and self-assured.

Trish said she lived with her husband, Kevin, and her two daughters. I couldn't wait to see the pictures of them that Trish promised to email me. Thankfully, technology meant that we didn't have to wait long to see what Trish and her family looked like. Obviously, I was most anxious to see how Trish herself looked. She mentioned that Kevin was a computer whiz and that he would scan some photographs and email them to me. Unfortunately, I didn't have a scanner, but I told her I would airmail pictures of the family as soon as possible. As we exchanged email addresses, we both commented on how dry our throats had become from talking so long. This was a very emotional time for us both, and I thought our conversation had gone really well. I gave Trish my phone number, and we said our goodbyes.

I had been on the phone for what seemed like hours and part of me still hadn't come to terms with what I had just done. Because there was neither the wait nor the expectation of my phone call, as there was with Maureen, it somehow felt completely different. I felt exhaustion and happiness but not quite the intense joy that I had felt when I first started on this journey with Maureen. I felt like a runner crossing the finishing line of a marathon, too exhausted to feel anything much.

Of course, I was amazed at the events but somehow, it seemed as if they were happening to someone else. In some ways they were, because I knew that these events had changed me irrevocably and made me into a new person. Not only had I gained two sisters, but my family life had changed because of it. It had become so much a part of my life these last few years that I could think of little else. I sometimes wondered if I was becoming too obsessed, too single minded with it all. Now that it was almost over, what was there to take its place?

As I looked up, Gord had a huge smile on his face. He had been listening to my side of the conversation, and he was obviously delighted with what he had heard. I was too tired and emotional to discuss much of what was said, so I just said that I would talk about it later, when we got home. The drive to our house gave me time to organize my thoughts and decide what I should do next. I thought I would call Tina after I had a hot bath to calm down and collect my thoughts. So, when we arrived home, I ran a bath and lay there; thinking what a strange journey it had been so far. I felt as though I had come a long way. I had felt like a big sister to Maureen and now, I felt as though I was becoming a little sister to Trish.

After my bath, I spoke to Gord about my conversation with Trish in more detail. He was also looking forward to meeting her one day soon. He told me that if I wanted to I could buy a ticket to England and be on the next flight. It was a great idea, and he was being his usual generous, thoughtful self, but I knew Trish wanted to come to Canada to meet her entire family, so I decided I would wait for her.

I called Tina and let her know the news. We spoke for almost an hour. I let her in on everything that was said in the conversation between Trish and me; all the little details and small pieces of information. She sounded really excited as I forewarned her that she should expect a call from Trish at any time since I had given Trish her number.

I then called Memère Rose and filled her in on my conversation with Trish. All she could say was how happy she was for me. She kept thanking me for searching for the two girls. I don't think she really understood the fact that they had registered as well and that's why there was a match in both instances. Anyhow, Memère Rose said that she hoped she could meet Trish when she came to meet us in Canada.

I thought a while and felt as though I should call Dad. It was a difficult decision because I could tell he still felt guilty about the whole situation. Just the thought of him being hurt by this whole thing made me stop and think. *Was I doing the right thing? Was I expecting too much of him? Was I pushing him too far?* I decided that he had a right to know. I should at least call him and tell him about the things that had transpired.

At this point, he wasn't even aware that there was another match at the agency. I thought that I had better let him know what was happening since, like me, Trish was a forceful person and was likely to ring him up one day. Maureen showed interest in meeting her birth father but since she was a shy girl, she would never have taken the initiative to call him. She was waiting for him to make the first move, which could take forever, while I knew Trish wouldn't just sit back and wait. Trish actually mentioned in our conversation that when she came to Canada she would want to meet *everyone* and that included her birth father.

I dialed his number and waited for him to answer, which he did after a couple of rings. I told him to sit down if he wasn't already and that I had incredible news. He went really quiet, and I actually felt sorry for him. I then just blurted out that I'd spoken with my eldest sister, that day. He didn't respond, so I started telling him about her; she had a wonderful life and felt thankful to her birth parents for giving her away. I knew this sounded insensitive and Trish really didn't say these words but I wanted him to know immediately that he didn't need to feel guilty for giving her away for adoption. He was aware that Maureen didn't have a great childhood and wasn't close to her parents. I think he felt badly for her so I wanted him to know that Trish's childhood was different and that he need not feel guilty. I then told him that Trish had a Ph.D. in chemistry, was married with two daughters, and lived in England. After I stopped speaking, there was silence for what seemed like minutes. I asked him what he thought about all of this and still he said nothing.

Finally, he spoke; he asked how she had ended up in England. I knew this fact would get him to speak. I told him about her family's various moves. Next, I mentioned how I thought Trish was quite forceful and that she reminded me of myself. Dad chuckled and then said he was happy for me. He was pleased that my search for my two sisters had such a positive outcome. I shared my feelings about Mom's involvement from up above, and he agreed in a shaky voice. I knew he was holding back tears.

Our conversation was going well, so I decided to say that Trish was thinking of coming over to Canada to meet us all. Suddenly, I heard the tone of his voice change. He told me that he didn't want to be part of all this, and that he certainly never thought he would meet his daughters. I could hear the guilt in his voice and could imagine the look on his face. For the second time in the same conversation I felt sorry for my Dad, who seemed scared of what his own family might think of him. He said how his hands had been tied, and that he had been feeling guilty and sad about it all these years. I told him that I had spoken to Memère Rose about this, and as far as everyone including myself was concerned, it was over. People do such things in their lives; they make decisions and some of them, they later regret.

He started talking about how close a relationship he had with his parents now and that they could never find out about the girls. He felt they were too old to understand, which I personally disagreed with. Even though they were old fashioned, they were wonderful people. Of course they would be shocked with the revelation, but they wouldn't react as severely as Dad anticipated they would. At this point though, I told him that he didn't need to tell them. I was just warning him that Trish might hunt him down when she came to Canada if he wouldn't agree to meet her. He didn't say too much after that. He didn't agree to meet her, but he didn't object either, which I thought was a little victory on my part.

I automatically included Maureen in the conversation. I figured that if Dad agreed to meet Trish then he would most likely meet Maureen as well. During the last year, he had never mentioned Maureen when I spoke to him. Maureen had been somewhat disappointed with his perceived lack of interest, but she didn't dwell on it. After all, she had two sisters and two brothers - and now, yet another sister - to be further acquainted with. However, I thought it was sad that he didn't want to meet the sister I had grown to love so much. It was a shame that he could not share in the family's joy at having suddenly expanded.

With Maureen on my mind, I decided to get off the phone with Dad and call her. I figured it would take him some time to digest the information I had just piled on him. I said I would call him when I knew of Trish's arrival date. He said that he would think about it, at which point, I expressed my wish to contact his brother and sister to arrange for them to meet Trish and Maureen, when Trish was in town.

Dad's sister, Tina, knew about the adoptions and was devastated when she found out about it, at around the same time as I had. We never spoke about it, so I wasn't even aware that she knew until after we met Maureen. I had no idea if Dad's brother knew anything, but I couldn't include his sister and not his brother. I hoped that Dad had the courage to at least speak with his siblings about the girls even if he couldn't, or wouldn't, speak with his parents.

I assured Dad once again, that much time had passed since the girls were given away; they were now women with lives and minds of their own. They didn't hold a grudge or feel resentful about the situation. I thought his mind seemed a little eased after hearing that. I put the phone down and felt confident that he would eventually want to meet both Maureen and Trish. Despite anything he might have thought about himself, Dad was a kind and good man. His emotions were not those of someone who didn't care; they were the emotions of a scared father not wanting, perhaps, to face the girls he thought he had so badly let down.

In my heart, I knew that the only way to overcome this was for all of them to meet. I resolved to try and make this happen.

The next morning, I went to the doctor again. I drove back home after seeing the doctor instead of going to work. My first priority was to speak to Maureen. I couldn't speak to her the night before because she was working the night shift. I hadn't spoken to my brothers yet either, but remembering their reaction to the news of Maureen, I felt that they could wait a little longer. Gord had already left for work, and the house seemed so peaceful. It actually felt good to sit alone and gather my thoughts before calling Maureen. I was nervous for some reason, and I hoped that Maureen would be as happy as I was.

I laughed at myself for staring at the telephone and being, yet again, too afraid to pick up the receiver. There had just been so many life changing phone calls recently. I picked up the receiver and dialed Maureen's number. When she didn't answer, I feared she wasn't home. But she answered on the third ring; her voice, clear and sweet.

We said our standard hellos, how are you, what's new, and so on. I then asked her if she had some time to talk. Alerted by this, she asked why. I told her that I had some wonderful and surprising news for her. She immediately responded by asking me if they had found our other sister. I couldn't believe that she had guessed what my news could be. It almost made me think that Tina had already spoken to her, but I knew she hadn't. With what had happened with Maureen a year ago, I suppose none of us had completely ruled out another big surprise.

I told Maureen about Lina's initial call concerning the match with Trish. Maureen listened quietly as I filled her in on the details. There was silence on the other end of the line. It turned out that Maureen had only been kidding when she guessed that there had been another match. After a few more seconds of silence, Maureen told me that she knew in her heart that they would find this other sister. I recalled Maureen's optimism and my pessimism about ever meeting our oldest sister.

Maureen asked me when I was going to write to Trish. She assumed that there would be similar procedures to the ones we had previously followed. I explained to her that since Trish and I had already spoken, there was no need for letter writing unless we wanted to. Maureen was surprised to hear that I had spoken with her already, and I felt bad for not filling her in on that bit of important information. I realized that I hadn't told Maureen any of this before, and I suddenly felt very guilty. She had, after all, perhaps more of a right to know what was going on than any of us.

She asked me how long I had known about the match. I explained that I had spoken with Lina only a couple of days ago, but that I had agonized about whether to wait to call Trish until after the confirmation of my pregnancy results in a couple of weeks. Maureen then asked how our conversation went, and I explained the details. Maureen laughed when I told her that Trish sounded aggressive and forward like me. She asked me when Trish might come here. I mentioned that Trish had indicated it could be in spring. I told Maureen how I felt that Trish might get here sooner than that. Trish had never been apart from her daughters so it would be difficult for her. Maureen was thrilled to hear she had two more nieces, and the rest of our conversation went really well. I told her that Trish's second given name was Maureen, and she laughed, surprised.

I also told Maureen that I had given Trish her phone number, and that she should expect a call any day now. I warned her that Trish was a little difficult to understand due to her accent, but Maureen didn't seem concerned about that. She was excited, just as Tina had been, about hearing from Trish. I hoped that Maureen would not be envious that Trish had a wonderful life with her adopted parents. I hoped that I was overreacting about how I thought Maureen would feel.

After I put the phone down, I thought about how different Trish and Maureen were from each other. They each displayed traits of my family; Trish for instance, was slightly headstrong like me, but Maureen was shy and retiring like Rocky. I suppose it brought home to me the different lives they must have led, and how life can be a lottery without you even knowing it. It was as if I were witnessing a social experiment before my very eyes.

Of course, both sisters had turned out great. I would not change them at all, but they each had their own little battle scars from the lives that they had led; each had her personal triumphs and disappointments etched into her character. I wondered if we were going to be able pull together as a family again and live a life that would include everyone and make them feel wanted.

My conversation with Maureen had made me feel guilty for not including her earlier. I felt as if I was treading a fine line between letting her know what was going on and making her feel as though I was talking about our "new" sister all the time.

I decided to call Rocky and tell him the news as well. We chatted about simple stuff for a couple of minutes before I sprang the news on him. I knew his reaction would be different this time around since he knew about the adoptions and had already met Maureen. But I was pleasantly surprised by how different the reaction really was. He asked me a pile of questions about Trish, and I tried to answer them as quickly as possible in order to keep the positive momentum going. Naturally, he was as shocked as my other siblings to find out that Trish lived in England. Rocky actually joked that it was great that he now had a place to stay when he traveled there.

I was pleased with Rocky's reaction, and I only hoped that Lenny's would be just as positive. Since Rocky and Lenny were presently living together, I told him that he could fill Lenny in on the situation if he wanted to.

I didn't go to work that day as I was exhausted with all the emotional turmoil. Maureen's and Rocky's reaction to the news exceeded my expectations, and I thanked God that they were happy. It was around 3 p.m. when Gord called me from work to tell me that we had received an email from Trish. He sounded excited as he told me that Trish looked a lot like Rocky, and that the eldest of her two girls was already blossoming into someone absolutely beautiful. I asked him if Trish looked like me at all. He said that there was a definite resemblance, which made sense since Rocky and I looked most alike, up until now that is. I wanted to get in my car and drive to the office, but Gord said he would print the photographs and bring them home for me. I asked him to hurry up.

The wait was absolutely excruciating. I was finally going to see what my eldest sister looked like. Every time I thought I heard the door open, I would rush out to see if it was Gord coming home with the photographs. Eventually he came home, and I grabbed the envelope from him and sat down at the kitchen table. My fingers were trembling as I took the pictures out. He had them printed on 5" x 7" sheets, so I could see everyone clearly. The first was a family photo of Trish, her husband Kevin, and the girls. My first reaction was that Trish looked like me, especially, in the upper part of the face.

Her daughters were absolutely beautiful, and the little one, Jennifer, resembled both Rocky and I when we were babies. The second picture was of Trish's eldest daughter, Sally-Ann, by herself. Gord wasn't exaggerating when he said that she was beautiful. She had the most stunning eyes I had ever seen. The next photograph was of little Jennifer alone. She was cute as a button with her blonde curly hair; she definitely had our family's genes.

I looked again at the picture of Trish; she really did look like Rocky. She had the same eyes and mouth. It was almost uncanny how they resembled each other. I thought that her face suited her personality. As I stared at Trish's picture all the emotion and the events of the last few years came flooding back. For the first time, I really thought of her as my eldest sister and felt comforted by that thought.

Again, I felt the guiding hand of Mom on my shoulder, and it felt good to have it there. The world was spinning and people were going about their ordinary daily business, but I felt as though the world had somehow changed slightly; that it was a warmer, better place. It made me more determined than ever to start a family of my own.

SISTERS REVEALED

8.
CLOSER AND CLOSER

The next day came quickly, and I ventured to the clinic again. This was probably going to be my last day of monitoring. With any luck, by tomorrow, I could start on the insemination process. When I reached work, I called Tina before emailing her the pictures sent in by Trish. I wanted to discuss the photos with her, but decided to hold back and let her call me after she had viewed them first.

I then called Rocky. He showed a lot of interest in the pictures so I emailed them to him as well. I mentioned to him that Trish could be his twin sister, and he chuckled. I don't think he took me seriously, but I knew that he would be as surprised as I was when he saw the pictures.

My phone rang, and it was Tina. She called to say that she had received the pictures and that I was right; Trish did look a lot like Rocky. She was almost screaming and yelling down the phone with excitement, and that made me excited too. We both thought Trish's daughters were cute and commented on how they looked like a great family. I asked if Tina thought that Trish looked anything like me, and she said she didn't. I must admit I was a little disappointed for not looking anything like either of our adopted sisters, but I suppose that's genes for you!

I heard another call coming through, so I asked Tina to hold the line as I thought it was most likely Rocky. It was Rocky, and all he said was, "I have a twin sister." I was quite surprised that he could see that Trish and he looked alike. Most people wouldn't be able see themselves in someone else. It proved just how much they truly looked alike. He also commented on Jennifer looking a lot like he did as a baby. I agreed with him but also added that she looked like me too.

Remembering that Tina was on the other line, I asked Rocky to hold while I said goodbye to Tina. When I returned to Tina, I was giggling and telling her how Rocky thought that Trish and he looked identical. I told her that I would speak with her later, and I went back to my call with Rocky. He asked me if I had sent any pictures to Trish. I told him that as soon as I obtained Trish's mailing address, I would be mailing her a black and white professional photograph of all the siblings with Shanelle, a black and white photograph of our parents in their twenties, and a recent picture of Maureen with Tina and me. I asked Rocky if he had spoken with Lenny yet. He said that he didn't see him last night, but he would print the photos and talk to him about it tonight; what a surprise for Lenny.

After Gord and I ate lunch, I decided to call Trish and discuss the pictures. I reached her voicemail, so I left my work number. She returned my call within half an hour, and I congratulated her on having such a beautiful family. I told Trish how much she looked like Rocky. She just laughed, thinking I was exaggerating, but I told her that even Rocky had called her his twin sister. She probably didn't want to hear that she looked like one of the boys, so I told her that I thought she resembled me as well. I mentioned how we all thought that her girls were beautiful and commented on Sally-Ann's eyes. Being the proud parent, Trish agreed that the picture of Sally-Ann was as fabulous as her beautiful eyes.

Trish gave me her home address, and I promised that I would mail the photographs of our family that day. She indicated that she and her in-laws would be anxiously awaiting them. In the meantime, she planned to call Tina and Maureen. Trish said that she would try and figure out who was who in the photographs, based on our personalities. Trish had mentioned her in-laws before; I could hear, from the tone of her voice, that they were close to her and had played an integral part in her search. Trish said that her mother-in-law kept crying when they found out that there was a match. Trish then admitted to shedding a few tears as well.

Trish and I spoke further about her and Kevin coming to Canada. She said that Kevin's mother would look after the girls when they came for a quick trip. I felt that it was probably a good idea to leave the girls at home not only because the girls were too young for a seven hour flight, but also because it was going to be an emotional trip for her. Trish didn't offer any time frame for her visit, but I felt, knowing Trish as I did, that it would be sooner rather than later.

I offered my home as a place for them to stay. However, if they preferred staying at a hotel, Gord and I would look after their hotel expenses. I felt it would perhaps be better for them to stay in a hotel during their first visit, allowing them a private space where Trish could react any way she liked without having us around her all the time. I filled her in on my conversations with Tina, Rocky, Maureen, Dad, and Memère Rose and how pleased they all were with the match. She said that she was looking forward to speaking to Tina and Maureen and asked for Lenny and Rocky's number. She also said that she would call again when she received the photographs and told me to take care.

I hurried to the post office and airmailed the photographs. The post office assistant told me that they would arrive in England within four to five working days. I felt glad that Trish would soon know what the whole family looked like and, perhaps, feel a part of things even though she was miles away.

Life seemed to speed up after I had talked to Trish on the phone; there was always someone asking me how it went, and I was forever re-telling my story. Most people's eyes fill with tears when they realize the enormity of my journey, and the coincidence and fate that had played a part along the way. Those who had already heard the story would ask how things were progressing and what the latest news was. Talking about adoptions made me realize that there were so many people who were adopted themselves, or knew people who adopted children. Some were searching for their birth parents or siblings and in some cases, were completely content with never looking for their birth family at all.

Every year, thousands of children are adopted into new families; they take on new lives, new names and new ways of being. However, the pull of the genetic bond is still strong; it may lie dormant for a while, perhaps even for years, but somehow, the desire to search out one's roots is ever present. This is what I found out from my sisters.

The journey for the birth family members is no less taxing than those of the adopted child. You are suddenly confronted with not only new siblings, but also a new way of looking at your parents. The life you thought you had turns out to be deceptive; the people you called your Mom and Dad turn out to have secrets and to have kept things from you for most of your life. This is a hard and bitter pill to swallow as trust is always something taken for granted in the relationship between parent and child.

I received a call from Trish at my workplace the following week. The first thing she said was, "What a beautiful family I have." I became misty-eyed as I heard Trish referring to us as her family; for

Trish to accept us as her family without even meeting us felt wonderful. I asked her if she had guessed which girl I was in the family photograph. She said that both she and her mother-in-law guessed that I was the girl on the right, in white. I told her that she had pointed out Tina, and that I was the girl on the left in the printed top. She seemed quite surprised which just seemed to prove that personalities don't necessarily match faces.

We laughed at the crazy mix-up before she commented on how much she really did look like Rocky. There was certainly no mix-up with the boys. She thought it was kind of spooky how the first born child and the last born child resembled one another the most. Then Trish went on about the long, curly, beautiful hair that Tina and I had; she said she got the short end of the stick where hair was concerned. She didn't think Maureen looked like any of the other siblings, with the possible exception of Lenny. I told her that Maureen looked most like Mom and Trish agreed. Trish thought our parents were so attractive, like movie stars. She also said both she and her mother-in-law thought Sally-Ann looked like Mom.

We talked a bit more before Trish told me the news: she and Kevin had starting making plans to travel to Toronto in January. I was so excited to hear this, and all I could think of was what a wonderful millennium year this was turning out to be. She indicated that they could only stay for a few days, but she wanted to meet as many family members as possible during that visit. I assured her not to worry and said that I would make it all happen. She decided to take me up on the offer to book them into a hotel for a few nights. Clearly, Trish agreed with me that at this point in our relationship, it would be best for them to stay in a neutral place. She asked me what the weather was going to be like and I just said, "Cold."

January is the coldest month in Toronto, when even Canadians start to feel the weather chill them to the bones. I decided not to tell this to Trish, as I did not want to put her off coming. I just advised her to pack lots of warm clothing. It was November now, and in a few short months, I would be meeting my oldest sister. I found that difficult to believe, and it was such a pleasant surprise that she wanted to meet us as much as we wanted to meet her.

After speaking with Trish, I felt a little panicky. I now had the task of convincing Dad to meet his two daughters. I didn't think it would be easy so I decided to use the Christmas season, with all the sentiments attached to it, to try and convince him. Trish didn't give me exact dates since she hadn't booked the flight yet, but I went ahead and checked the prices of hotel suites around the airport.

There was something momentous in the thought of the whole family coming together like this; it was as if some great energy was pulling us together. I knew no one else shared my view of the situation, but it was difficult not to think in such a way after all the coincidences. I never once had the feeling that I was not doing the right thing. I had sometimes wondered if it was all going to work out, but an inner light had always guided me in whatever I was doing; the light of Mom.

The next couple of weeks went by quickly. During all the chaos, I kept feeling like I was pregnant, but unfortunately my test indicated that I wasn't. It was only my first attempt so I wasn't that disappointed. I never really expected that it would happen quickly. I couldn't try in the month of December because of the Christmas holidays; my next attempt had to be in January. January was looking like a very busy month. I couldn't think of a better way to usher in the millennium than meeting my eldest sister for the first time. It also occurred to me that it would be great to have a millennium baby.

Between shopping for Christmas presents and making plans for Trish's visit, the month of December flew by. Trish finalized her flight dates and I booked the hotel suite for them. They would be arriving on the 27th of January, 2000, so it was time to try and convince Dad to meet the girls. I was planning a party at my house, and I decided to invite Dad's sister and brother so he would feel like he had no choice but to turn up. I hated using these tactics, but it just wouldn't seem right if he missed the opportunity to meet Trish while she was here.

Christmas Eve was being held at Aunt Linda's again. We agreed to go to her place because we wanted to see Memère Rose and Leandre, who were also going to be there, and we didn't want to create any tension for our grandparents to deal with. Memère Rose felt horrible that she wouldn't be seeing Maureen and Megan again, but if she wasn't able to see the rest of her grandchildren it would have been very hurtful to her. Tina and I, again, made plans to visit Maureen before dinner at Aunt Linda's house. Rocky said he wanted to join us as well, and I knew this would thrill Maureen.

A few days before Christmas Eve, I received my first Christmas card from Trish. It wasn't a "Sister" card, but I didn't really expect it to be. It touched my heart immensely to know that she was thinking of me. I had sent her a card as well, and I hoped she received it on time. With the few conversations we had and the little things we did share, I started realizing how similar Trish and I were. I couldn't wait to meet her in January.

I received a beautiful card from Maureen with the words, "To my sister and brother-in-law." She loved Gord, and I was so glad that she included him in her most beautiful message to us. Maureen is a very sentimental person just like Mom was, and the words she wrote brought tears to my eyes.

Christmas Eve came and went; it was a terrible shame that we did not spend it with Maureen, who I knew would have loved to have been there to share in the family festivities. But she said she understood.

However, I knew Maureen's spirits would be lifted as soon as I told her my news about Dad. I had spoken to him over Christmas, and to my surprise he had said yes; he wanted to meet both of his daughters. At first, I thought that I was not hearing him right, but he repeated it; he wanted to meet Trish and Maureen in the New Year.

I told him that he wouldn't regret his decision, and that he owed it to his daughters and himself to at least meet them. I knew that it was overwhelming and scary for him, but I felt that once he met his daughters, he would feel a sense of relief and more importantly, closure. I felt that if the girls themselves told him that they both understood the reasons for being given away and held no resentment, it would relieve him of some of his guilt. Now I prayed that Dad wouldn't change his mind before January 27th.

It was the new millennium. All over the world, people were celebrating new beginnings and perhaps hoping for a newer, brighter world. I was certainly sharing in the cheer as my family members phoned each other and wished each other a happy New Year.

I didn't think I was the only person who expected the world to be different at the dawn of the new year; in fact, I suppose most people did. But with the visit of Trish and the chance of a pregnancy, I hoped that perhaps my new world would happen a little sooner than everyone else's.

The month of January was going by so quickly, and I felt like I was running on pure adrenaline. I was regretting not waiting until February to make another pregnancy attempt, but I persevered. I managed to make all the necessary arrangements for Trish's visit, and my entire family was very much looking forward to meeting our sister from England. The family members on Dad's side were also looking forward to meeting Maureen since they hadn't had the chance previously. I started feeling a little bad for Maureen; it probably appeared as if everyone wanted to meet Trish, whereas some hadn't even made an attempt to meet Maureen in the past year.

Regrettably, my concerns were validated. Maureen confided in me that she felt like everyone was welcoming Trish with open arms and going out of their way for Trish, when they hadn't done the same for her. I reminded her that she had not wanted to meet the family all at once. It was also a new experience for the family, which understandably shocking and nerve-wracking to deal with. It was different with Trish only because we had already experienced it a year ago with Maureen. Everyone was calmer and, more importantly, more accepting of the news about Trish. I told Maureen that with Trish living in England, it was exciting to think that she was traveling thousands of miles just to meet us. I told Maureen that I had been so nervous to meet her, and that I was more anxious than nervous to meet Trish. With Maureen being such a fragile person, I tried to be more sensitive to her feelings; especially when it came to Trish.

Trish and Kevin were due to arrive at 1:30 p.m. on Thursday, 27th of January, 2000 and return to England on the 30th of January. I booked the hotel for three nights. The family party at my house was planned for Friday, and I made dinner reservations at one of my favorite French restaurants in downtown Toronto, Le Papillon, for Saturday night. On Sunday, Gord and I planned to take Trish and Kevin downtown to the beautiful shops that Toronto offered. The only question that remained unanswered was when Dad would meet the girls. My plan was to invite him to my house for the family party, which included his sister and brother. It was my hunch that he would want to meet the girls before everyone arrived.

When I spoke with Dad's sister, Aunt Tina, she thanked me for including her and added that she would speak with her brother, Mario, about the party. She also said that she would speak with Dad about everything. I detected sadness in her voice when she spoke about Dad meeting his daughters for the first time. I also became emotional when I thought about their first meeting. I just hoped that he would actually have the courage to go through with it.

I could not bear the thought of Dad backing out at this stage. I knew it was a hard decision for him to make and an even harder process for him to go through, but I felt as if he owed his daughters this meeting. After all these years, this was perhaps the only way to offer some recompense, and to finally give them the love they deserved.

It was only a few days before Trish and Kevin's arrival, and I was becoming a nervous wreck. I wanted Memère Rose to meet Trish so badly, but it seemed that she wasn't going to be able to make it because Leandre wasn't capable of driving that far. Aunt Linda had decided that she couldn't meet the girls, because she still wasn't prepared to tell her husband about them. I just didn't know what to do. If Memère Rose didn't meet Trish this time round, who knew when she'd ever get the opportunity again, especially since Memère Rose was old and Trish lived so far away. Gord could see my dilemma and being the wonderful husband that he was, he took matters into his own hands and decided to arrange for one of our co-workers to pick up Memère Rose and bring her to our home. She could sleep over at our place for the night and get a lift back to her home, from the same co-worker, the following day. I couldn't thank Gord enough for being so thoughtful and making my life so much easier.

I breathed a little easier knowing that the issue of Memère Rose was finally resolved. However, Dad in the meantime had decided not to answer my calls. There seemed to be one problem after another. I called and called, but still I could not get to speak with him. Finally, I left a detailed message about the itinerary for Trish's visit on his answering service. I also mentioned that his sister and brother would be meeting the girls on the Friday. I suggested he come early if he wanted to meet them first. I hoped that my message would elicit a response.

Trish sounded so pumped up about the whole experience when I spoke to her on the Wednesday before her arrival. I could tell that she was a hyperactive and excitable person. I told her I would be meeting her and Kevin at the airport by myself, and that they need not worry about having to drive for their entire trip. She seemed relieved to hear that, since it would probably have taken their entire stay to get used to driving on the opposite side of the road. Tina was going to take the day off work and accompany me to the airport, but I didn't tell Trish, since Tina and I had decided to keep it a surprise. Trish and I said our goodbyes. I wished them a safe journey and excitedly said, "I'll see you tomorrow!"

I invited Maureen to come to the airport with Tina and me, but she had to work. However, even if she could have had the day off work, traveling to the airport would have been an issue; she still didn't have her driver's license and Tina and I didn't have time to pick her up. Maureen was a little disappointed since she would have loved to share the experience with us. But she was consoled by the fact that she would meet Trish at my house the next day.

That was it; things were in place. I had done all I could to make the trip a success. It was now left to everyone else. I suddenly became very emotional; in only a matter of hours, I would be meeting my new sister. That night, I virtually lied awake the whole night, mulling over things in my head. Everything that had happened in the last few years had left me feeling drained, yet strangely excited; it was as if I was moving towards some ultimate goal that was coming to an end, and it was an unsettling thought. There is a theory that those who are in accidents or on the battlefields, hold on to their lives just long enough to see home, and after they do, they die. It is the goal that keeps them alive; it is the vision of the end that drives them forward.

This was how I felt as I lay in bed thinking of Trish. For so long, it seemed, it had been my goal to re-unite the family, and it looked as though this would happen tomorrow. After that, what would happen? Would we all disappear into our own lives again? Would we form one happy unit, or would we go the way of so many other families and merely exist from day to day, letting each other slip away again? I turned over and tried to sleep - far away, in the UK, Trish was preparing for her flight.

SISTERS REVEALED

9.
TRISH'S REUNION

I woke up, and it was freezing outside. It was sunny but minus twenty degrees Celsius, and all I could think about was Trish and Kevin's reaction to the bitter cold. They rarely experience freezing temperatures like ours in England, but when I warned them about our cold weather they didn't seem bothered. I threw on a sweater and jeans, and my warmest coat.

Gord and I drove to work together, and Tina picked me up at 10:30 a.m. We went to a mall close by and decided to buy a vase and flowers for Trish. She could put them in her hotel room and hopefully, it would make her room seem homier. We attempted to eat lunch but we were both so nervous that we could barely get anything down. After lunch, we drove to the airport. It was a little early, but we couldn't stand the anticipation any longer. We parked the car and found the arrival gate that they would be coming from. Tina and I checked the arrival times on the television screen, every ten minutes or so, to see if the flight had arrived. My stomach was performing cartwheels, and it felt worse than being on a first date; at least, in my vague recollection of what a first date felt like.

The airport was its usual busy self. People were coming and going; everywhere, there were faces either tired or excited, and children ran through people's legs, bumping into those who waited. There was an air of expectancy to the building that I had never before experienced; everyone seemed to be in on the journey that Tina and I were making. Small, inconsequential details took on new meaning as I tried to take my mind off things. I noticed that the arrivals board seemed to have slowed down to an almost standstill; its information being held from us for precious seconds.

I checked the screen at 1:30 p.m., the time the plane was scheduled to land, and to my surprise, it had arrived. For some reason, I hadn't expected it to be exactly on time. I started feeling emotional; in just minutes, I would be hugging my oldest sister for the first time.

Having Tina with me would actually make me more emotional since I would be witness to her tears and emotions as well.

Tina and I couldn't look at each other anymore since we were both becoming a blubbering mess. Our eyes were becoming puffy from the overuse of our tear ducts. It was evident to the people around us that not only were we waiting for someone, but that we were becoming very emotional.

The crowd increased and we heard English accents from the passengers crossing the gate. There was a lot of hugging and kissing going on, and it took all my strength not to start bawling. Tina and I positioned ourselves so we could see Trish and Kevin as soon as they passed the gate.

Many people were walking through the arrivals gate, but we still didn't see Trish. Tina and I grew concerned thinking that maybe we had missed them, or worse, hadn't recognized them. We finally had something to laugh about since the thought of not recognizing our own sister was crazy.

Suddenly, we spotted them walking through the gate - they didn't see us, which was how we kind of wanted it - and my heart nearly pounded out of my chest. Tina just kept saying, "Oh my God," and the first words that came out of my mouth when I saw Trish from a distance was, "She looks like me." Trish and Kevin had to walk through an aisle that was roped off on both sides, and we were right at the end waiting for them. It seemed to take an eternity for them to reach us, and I was crying before she even saw us. I didn't dare look at Tina since I knew she'd be crying as well.

In that one instant everything I had been working for came together; all the phone calls, the worrying, the biting of nails. It all converged into this moment where our family united for the first time ever; the siblings that had lived their whole lives together and the two sisters who were only revealed a few years ago.

We waved to Trish, and she came running to us. She hugged and kissed us both. She had tears in her eyes as well, although, she was a lot more composed than Tina and I. Trish started going on about our hair and how beautiful it was. I noticed that she looked like a combination of Aunt Tina and me. More than that, however, Trish was almost Rocky's double.

Trish told Tina that it was a wonderful surprise to meet her here. Tina was actually shocked that I hadn't revealed our plans since I wasn't the best at keeping silly secrets. At this point, we were just chatting away and had completely forgotten about poor Kevin. Trish finally introduced us to him, and we gave him a hug. Once I took my eyes away from Trish, I realized that people were staring at us and smiling. If they only knew that we had just met a full blood sister for the first time, I'm sure they'd be emotional as well. In fact, part of me wanted to announce our meeting to everyone in the airport. It was difficult to contain my overwhelming happiness.

We hugged again and let the emotion wash over us in waves. All the tension had left the atmosphere of the airport, and it now seemed a place of happiness and togetherness; it had suddenly transformed from a place that parted people into a place that brought people together.

We left the airport and drove to the hotel. Tina, Trish, and I started talking about clothes and the coats we were wearing. It seemed odd but I was thankful we were communicating easily; there didn't seem to be any tension or awkwardness.

Tina parked the car while Trish and Kevin went to check in. While they were checking in, Kevin pulled out his camera and snapped a picture of Trish and me. Our faces were red from the freezing cold air and we were sniffling, but I didn't care since this would be our first picture together, and I cherished it.

We waited for Tina to return before going up to the hotel room and settling them in. The room was plain but spacious. Trish put water in the vase and arranged the flowers we had bought her. They definitely gave the room a little character, and she thanked us. I was looking at Trish now without her coat, and I noticed how slim she was, her legs in particular. We all had long legs for our height and short torsos. I made a comment to Trish about her long slim legs. I said that I was jealous since my thighs were bigger. She laughed and agreed but thought she wasn't nearly as thin as Tina. That's when Kevin stepped in, and while looking at Tina he said, "That girl needs a good meal." We all laughed. I was happy to see us all getting along so easily, so quickly.

We didn't stay in the room for long because Trish and Kevin were starving and we were meeting Gord at The Keg Restaurant. We decided to walk, since it was only across the street from the hotel, but we nearly froze to death. On our walk, Trish and Kevin kept saying how "bloody freezing" our city was. Gord was already waiting for us, and he and Trish hugged each other immediately. They had spoken to one another over the phone and had already developed a connection; so naturally, they showed affection towards one another. Kevin and Gord shook hands, and we sat at a table.

We chatted about our jobs, their flight here, their children and how the weekend would hopefully unfold. We had a few drinks and munchies, but Kevin ordered the largest steak on the menu, since he had missed beef after Mad Cow Disease became prevalent in England. We all couldn't believe how a man Kevin's size could consume such a large meal and still love every minute of it. It was fun just watching the two of them and listening to their accents. Tina's boyfriend Steve soon arrived and joined our table. He was very interested in meeting Trish and thought this whole adoption experience was surreal. Steve had actually never met his birth mother since she left him with his dad at birth, so he was hoping to one day locate her and go through a similar process.

I couldn't help but stare at Trish and feel overwhelmed by the fact that my oldest sister was sitting next to me; she was so similar to me, not only in the slight physical resemblance, but in her personality as well. When I met Maureen for the first time, all I could see was Mom. With Trish, I saw myself and Dad's side of the family. It occurred to me that it was odd, that the two girls who were given away for adoption were the most similar to my parents. The rest of us, I felt were more a combination of our parents.

The talk was easy and relaxed, but we did not stay too long because Kevin and Trish had traveled for over ten hours, and with the time difference, they were wiped out. The next day was Friday - the day that Trish would meet the rest of the family. I was still not sure whether Dad would come; it had been a while since I had spoken to him, and I was unsure if he had received my message.

It was yet another restless night, and I couldn't get my mind off the party and how I wanted everything to turn out perfectly for Trish and Maureen. I prayed that Dad would keep his word and meet his two oldest daughters. I was also very excited for Memère Rose since she hadn't thought she would be able to meet Trish, but she was now, thanks to Gord. When I called Memère Rose earlier that week to advise her of our plan to get her to my house, she was deliriously happy and thankful. She always reminded me of what a wonderful husband I had in Gord and that I should never forget it.

Every time I closed my eyes, I saw Trish's face that reminded me so much of my own. I was beside myself with happiness; it had all gone according to plan. I thought of my eldest sister just a few miles away and smiled to myself in the stillness of the night. Everything was quiet; the moon was out and the world seemed hushed as it bathed in the magical, silver light. I looked skywards and let my eyes defocus in the darkness of the room. I knew that I was being cared for still, that someone was pulling the strings to make all these amazing events happen, and I knew who it was. I smiled. "Thanks Mom," I said, and fell asleep.

I bounced out of bed on Friday morning and even though I only had a few hours of real sleep, I still had a lot of energy. I was sure that it was from the sheer excitement of what was going to happen today.

I picked up Kevin and Trish at 11 a.m. as planned, and we went to my place of business where Gord was waiting for us. Gord and I took them to an Italian restaurant named Via Allegro for lunch, and they absolutely loved both the food and the atmosphere. We drank a little wine, and Kevin had a couple of beers. We had pictured Kevin to be some uptight scientist, but we couldn't have been further from the truth. He was so much fun and such a brilliant man to converse with. I noticed that Gord and Kevin were getting along great, and the four of us were definitely bonding well together. Kevin was fascinated with Gord's new Corvette as most men would be, so we decided that Kevin should spend the next few hours with Gord while Trish and I stayed together. I thought it was a splendid idea since it would give me some alone time with my sister.

We went to a mall directly across the street from the restaurant where we had lunch. We didn't have a lot of time, but I wanted to show Trish my favorite store to buy clothes and shoes. It was around 3 p.m. when I realized that we had better head home; I still had to pick up the food and Memère Rose was due to arrive at around 4 p.m. Everyone else was due to arrive at 6 p.m. I was actually looking forward to picking up the food since the owners of the local specialty shop were friends and were aware of the reasons for the party. They wanted to meet Trish badly, but I didn't want Trish to feel like some trophy prize so I asked her first if she felt comfortable meeting them. She excitedly said that she wanted to meet anyone who was part of my life.

We walked into the store and I introduced them. My friends felt that not only did we look alike, but that Trish's demeanor was similar to mine as well. We stayed and chatted for a few minutes but unfortunately, time wasn't on our side. Memère Rose would be arriving soon, and I started getting emotional again at the thought of Trish meeting her for the first time.

Gord and Kevin were already home when we arrived. I gave Trish and Kevin a little tour of our house and they thought it was really nice. They explained that they had bought a new house in England and were planning on moving in during the spring. They talked about the small differences between the two countries as we walked round the house; they told me that in the UK, room sizes were a lot smaller and very few houses had basements. I felt proud to show my house to my big sister. She seemed so interested in what I was saying that time just flew by, and I lost track of time altogether.

Suddenly, I heard the doorbell ring and realized with a start that it must be Memère Rose. I ran to the door while Trish stayed in the family room with Gord and Kevin. Memère Rose and I hugged, and she asked for some water right away since her throat was so dry from talking with the nice young man who drove her to our house. I thought it was funny and had no idea what a seventy-seven year old lady and a twenty-two year old man had to talk about, but I was pleased that she had a nice, safe drive. I sensed that Memère Rose was nervous, so I took her to the spare bedroom where she would be sleeping that night so she could unpack her bag. We were in the room talking for about five minutes when I thought that Trish might take Memère Rose's absence as a negative reaction, so I asked Memère Rose if she was ready to meet Trish. Memère Rose looked at me with her eyes wide open and said, "Oh! She's here now?" I laughed and was relieved that I could explain to Trish why it took us so long to come downstairs.

Memère Rose went straight to Trish and gave her a big hug. Trish's smile was unbreakable. She said, "Hi Rose!" as she hugged Memère Rose. There weren't really any tears, with the exception of mine. Memère Rose explained how she didn't think she'd have been able to meet Trish if her nice grandson-in-law hadn't made it happen. Memère Rose told Trish that she had a wonderful slim figure. Once I noticed them talking more, I left them alone and busied myself in the kitchen.

When alone with my thoughts, I couldn't help comparing Maureen and Trish's first introductions to Memère Rose and how different they had been. Memère Rose and Maureen clicked instantly, but with Trish, it seemed somewhat uncomfortable. Then I realized that Maureen wanted a mother figure so badly in her life and Memère

Rose would be the closest fit since Mom was gone, which probably affected the initial meeting. I also remembered that Maureen had called Memère Rose, "Memère" when they first met, while Trish called her, "Rose."

All these thoughts were going through my head because I wanted Trish to be as close to Memère Rose as Maureen had become, and I didn't know how I could help her. I knew I was being unrealistic since Trish loved her parents dearly and would probably never refer to Memère Rose as her grandmother, mostly due to her mother being almost the same age as Memère. Nor would she ever refer to Dad as her father, since she already had a father whom she loved very much. I felt that Trish wanted, more than anything, to be close to her siblings since she had never known any until now.

I suppose what Trish and Maureen wanted from this experience came down to their varying personalities. If I have learnt one thing from my journey, it is that people react to things in remarkably different ways, and that there is no such thing as a typical reaction. This is undoubtedly due to the way that we are brought up; we come to expect, want, and need different things. Maureen wanted the mother figure she so desperately needed all her life, and Trish wanted to know, for her own peace of mind, where she had come from. This created two entirely separate scenarios.

I have often asked myself what I wanted to achieve from this. I find it difficult to answer; perhaps I wanted a sense of truth or perhaps just a sense of family. But whatever it was, as I stood in the kitchen listening to Memère Rose and Trish talking and laughing in the other room, I felt like I had done it, at least for now.

I started towards the family room and heard Memère Rose explaining to Trish the reasons for giving her away for adoption. My heart was aching for my Memère Rose because I knew she felt partly responsible for the adoptions. However, she wanted the girls to know why. She wanted them to try and understand her husband's state of health and her own at the time. Trish repeatedly told her that it was okay, and that she had a wonderful life and held no animosity towards Memère Rose or her birth parents.

The doorbell rang and it was Tina and Shanelle. Trish gave Shanelle a hug and told her how beautiful she was, and how she sort of looked like her eldest daughter, Sally-Ann. I noticed that Trish looked more comfortable once Tina had arrived.

About half an hour later, the doorbell rang again and it was Lenny and Rocky. This was the second time in a year that they would be meeting a new sister. Rocky had already seen pictures of Trish and thought they looked very much alike, so when he entered the family room where Trish was, he asked, "Where's my twin?" I thought it was a fabulous icebreaker and Trish ran over, and hugged and kissed him. Then she gave Lenny a big hug and a kiss. Tina and I had tears in our eyes all over again. Trish and Rocky kept staring at one another in disbelief at how much they truly looked alike. It seemed easier for all of us the second time around since we had experienced it before; the uncertainties and complete shock were not present. We had a year to get to know Maureen and deal with the fact that we had two sisters who were given away. We now welcomed the second sister to complete our family.

The photo albums didn't take long to come out. Trish had never seen pictures of us siblings as children, and she couldn't wait to see if we looked similar growing up. We laughed at our appearances as we sifted through quite a few years. Our changing hairstyles were a riot, and Tina's huge glasses that she wore in high school were way too funny. I loved the eighties, but the styles were certainly bold.

We were all getting along famously, and Kevin was videotaping everything so that we would never forget a single second. Suddenly, the phone rang. It was Aunt Tina. She said she was on her way to pick up her brother, Mario, and wanted to let me know that they'd be arriving shortly. I could hear the tension in her voice. Aunt Tina wanted to meet my sisters but was very nervous for Dad. She placed a lot of the blame on Memère Rose and had expressed her feelings about how she thought my parents were robbed of knowing their first two children. It made Aunt Tina feel very sad that my parents were forced to give the girls away. I didn't argue with her even though I was very defensive of Memère Rose. I understood where Aunt Tina was coming from and it made sense that she would defend her brother, but I had reminded her that we were not there when it happened and that maybe if Dad had told his parents they could have helped out. The support of two families would have been a lot better than relying on an ill family to take on all the responsibilities.

It was around 7:30 p.m. when Aunt Tina and Uncle Mario arrived. I could see the anguish in my aunt's eyes as she walked in. I told her that Maureen still hadn't arrived but to come and meet Trish. They both hugged their new niece and couldn't believe how much she resembled their family. Trish certainly was her father's daughter and oddly enough, the three of them clicked immediately. Trish, Aunt Tina, and Uncle Mario sat around the kitchen table eating munchies and chatting. The three of them sat and talked for quite awhile. We left them on their own as we knew that they would want to tell Trish about her birth father and their family.

It was now almost 8:30 p.m. and we were all growing very concerned about Maureen. She hadn't called and was now over two hours late. Could she have decided not to come? As this thought raced through my mind, I realized it didn't make sense as this was a big night for Maureen. She was meeting her sister, her aunt, and her uncle for the first time. I started to feel very concerned that she might have had an accident on the way. The weather was still excruciatingly cold, and the roads were quite treacherous at this time of year. I started to wish that she would turn up, just so that I would know she was OK.

Just as I began thinking that Maureen had decided not to show up, the doorbell rang. I ran to open the door. Maureen had tears in her eyes, and she was shaking as she explained that they'd got lost because Paul wouldn't listen to her. I empathized with her since she was already under tremendous stress. I took her coat and pulled her aside for a minute so she could catch her breath and calm down a bit. I gave her a big hug and asked if she was ready. She kept apologizing for being late, so I just hugged her and told her not to worry. I said, "Let's get this initial part over with." Maureen was totally looking forward to meeting Trish, but she was more nervous than excited at meeting her birth father's family. I couldn't blame her since it appeared as though they had no interest in her until now.

Megan and Paul had already started mingling when I brought Maureen out to meet Trish. Again, my emotions got the better of me and by now, I was exhausted. Trish and Maureen hugged one another and spoke briefly while Tina, Lenny and Rocky all gave Maureen a hug. Maureen then noticed Memère Rose and ran to her. They truly had a special bond, and I was glad that Memère Rose was present to see our entire family, with the exception of our father, together for the very first time. All of her dear daughter's children were finally together.

Maureen made her way to Aunt Tina and Uncle Mario who had been watching the commotion in the family room. They both hugged her and told her how nice it was to meet, at last. My aunt was extremely emotional with both girls, but seemed on the verge of tears after hugging Maureen. I asked her if she was okay, and she asked me for a drink. She looked extremely pale and I poured her a glass of red wine. Aunt Tina shook her head in disbelief and finally managed to say, "My God! Maureen does look like your mother!"

We all agreed that it was like having Mom in the room with us which made us feel a bond that we had perhaps never felt before in our lives. There was only one person missing, and that was Dad. I was still waiting for him to call so that we would know if he was coming. Every few minutes or so I would expect the phone to ring, but it never did. I caught myself thinking that perhaps there was a fault, perhaps the line was dead, and perhaps there was a problem at his end. But it was stupid to think that. It was obvious that he was just not going to phone.

It was around 9:30 p.m. when Aunt Tina and Uncle Mario suggested we call our father and try to convince him to come over. I personally didn't think it was a great idea since there were too many people; however, I went along with the suggestion. Thankfully, he answered on the second ring.

I had some privacy for a moment, so I asked him why he hadn't called and if he had a change of heart. He said that he was willing to meet them tomorrow morning at the hotel. I gave him the hotel name and Trish's room number. He said to expect him at 10 a.m. Dad then reiterated that he would meet them but did not want to be part of any other plans during the weekend. He said he couldn't promise what would happen after they met, but he would at least meet them once. He sounded nervous and emotional as he spoke, and there was still a hint of uncertainty in his voice. I just felt pleased for Maureen and Trish that he wasn't backing out.

Aunt Tina spoke to him before I hung up. I could hear her trying to convince him to come over right away, and suddenly, everyone was screaming, "Yeah! Come over now!" I had really hoped to avoid this kind of situation, as I knew that it would make Dad feel awkward. I didn't want anything to change his mind about meeting Maureen and Trish. I didn't know what the rest of their conversation was about, but Aunt Tina informed us that he wouldn't be coming over that night.

I spoke with Maureen and Trish and confirmed Dad's plans with them. Maureen and Paul had rented a hotel room near Trish's hotel for two nights, so they didn't have to travel back and forth all weekend. It also allowed them to spend more time with Trish due to the time not wasted on travel.

Everyone started leaving at around 11 p.m., which was a little early for our family, but we were all so emotionally drained. Furthermore, tomorrow was going to be another huge day for Maureen and Trish; they were only eleven hours away from meeting their birth father.

After everyone left, Gord gave me a huge hug and helped clean up. Memère Rose went to bed before Gord and I. We stayed up talking about the day's events, and how well everything went, and I became emotional again. It was something Gord was getting used to, but he still questioned me. I told him that I was just thinking about how the meeting with Dad and my sisters was going to unfold tomorrow.

I was ambiguous towards Dad's actions. On the one hand, I understood and respected his feelings; this was an enormous challenge for him and one that he was uncertain of. On the other hand, he had two daughters who wanted to see him. They wanted to see him because they needed to know where they had come from; it was not to accuse him or suggest that he had done anything wrong, but to mend wounds and heal scars.

I knew he never wanted to give them away for adoption, and I was almost positive he never imagined meeting them. I wondered what was going through his mind right now. He was guaranteed a sleepless night, and he was surely praying to God to give him strength to get through the next day. I was quite certain he was thinking of Mom right now, and how much he loved her when they had conceived the two beautiful girls that he was about to meet. It saddened me that he had to do this alone and without his wife by his side. Mom's death had left him devastated. Now he had to face this alone, but I felt that had she still been alive, we would never have met Maureen and Trish in the first place.

I often pondered about the prospect of my parents telling us about the adoptions, had Mom survived. Personally, I didn't think it would have happened. I still thought that this unbelievable experience and truly remarkable miracle of circumstances was a gift from Mom, from up above. We all felt a connection with Maureen and now Trish, and our family was whole, or at least after tomorrow, it would be.

SISTERS REVEALED

10.
THE FINAL MEETING

Gord woke me up at 10 a.m., and I thanked him for letting me sleep in. Apparently, I was tossing and turning all night. I had my usual breakfast consisting of oatmeal and coffee and realized that at that very moment, Dad was with his two daughters for the first time in his life. I wondered how it was going at Trish's hotel. It was now 10:30 a.m., and I wanted to call Trish's room so badly, but I knew that I couldn't disturb them.

When my phone rang, I jumped up and quickly reached for the receiver. It was Tina, and I could barely make out what she was saying with all the background noise. She asked me to add one more person to tonight's dinner reservations, and that it was Dad who wanted to join us. "Of course," I said to Tina, thinking to myself that everything must have gone really well. Tina cheerfully announced that apparently the meeting was very emotional, but that they all seemed happy and that Dad wanted to spend the day with them.

I cried after hanging up with Tina, and Gord asked me what was wrong. I told him that absolutely nothing was wrong, and that I was crying tears of joy. I somehow knew that when Dad met Trish and Maureen, that he wouldn't be able to just walk away and never see them again.

I called the restaurant and informed them of the changes to the dinner reservations. I was walking on air for the rest of the day. The final piece of the jigsaw had fallen into place, and I felt as though I could relax for the first time in years. I wanted to tell my whole family how much I loved them, and how happy I was that we had been brought together in such a way that, if nothing else, Mom would be smiling upon us as she so obviously wanted to, during her lifetime.

When Gord and I arrived at the restaurant that night, everyone was already seated. We weren't late; they were all early. I went around the table and hugged everyone. I couldn't wait to speak with Trish and Maureen and hear about their meeting with Dad. When Dad saw me, he came rushing over and gave me a big hug. He looked at me through swollen eyes and all he could say was, "Thank you." I then thanked him for not backing out and for having the courage to meet his daughters. I told him that Mom would have been proud of him, and we both became teary eyed. Then, to change our emotional conversation, I blurted out, "They're not such bad girls, eh?" He laughed and said that they were both beautiful; he thought Trish resembled his family and that he was startled when he first laid eyes on Maureen because, she looked so much like Mom.

I left Dad to hug Trish. She said that Dad was a complete basket case when they met and that she would tell me the details later.

Champagne was brought over to the table; it was a gift from the owners of the restaurant. Dad began the toast by welcoming Maureen and Trish into our family and commented on how nice it was to meet them. I couldn't help but add to it by saying that our family was now complete with our dear mother who, I felt, was watching over us right now with a big smile on her face. Everyone toasted, and most of us had teary eyes. I held back the urge to ball my eyes out with both sadness and joy; sadness because I missed Mom terribly and wished she was alive to be with us tonight, and joy because all six siblings were finally together with Dad.

After ordering our meals, Trish asked for everyone's attention. She took a present out of a bag she had hidden under the table and handed it to me. I asked her what it was for, and she said that Maureen, Tina and herself, had bought it to thank me for arranging this entire weekend and more importantly, for being responsible for Maureen and herself meeting their birth family. I felt a little embarrassed as I opened the gift, but I was thankful. It was a beautiful soapstone coaster set with subtle dragonflies etched into it. It was absolutely gorgeous. I thanked my sisters and told them it was unnecessary.

The dinner went beautifully and everyone loved their meals. At one point in the evening, Dad stood between Trish and me, and bent down to whisper in Trish's ear, "You know Debbie made this happen?" Trish agreed with him and patted his hand while I blushed. He looked at me and said that I was a beautiful person. Maybe our newfound sisters would bring our family closer together. Only time would tell.

I looked around the table, at all the smiling faces, and felt the world stop for a second. Suddenly, it was as if someone had pressed a button and the screen had paused, and I was left floating, alone in the crowd. I noticed the dim lines of genetic connectivity that joined person to person, and perhaps for the first time, saw my own self as not merely an individual, but part of a chain that stretched far back into our family's past. I desperately wanted to be a part of its future as well, but that was out of my hands for the moment.

Dad looked happy and relaxed now, as did his daughters who had each made such efforts to be there. The notion of family is perhaps, not contained in the large and grand commitments like holidays or birthdays, but in the small, yet significant sidelines of life: the resemblance in a laugh, the shared character traits, and the moments of understanding.

As suddenly as it had paused, the room sprung back into life. I was back in the crowd and we laughed, drank, and ate into the night, all of us becoming more comfortable with each other, like a family should.

The next morning, I awoke with mixed emotions. I was thrilled at how my entire family was bonding with our adopted sisters, but I wondered what would happen next. Would Dad stay involved in Trish and Maureen's life? Would he be closer to the rest of us now? Was this just a fantasy weekend; one that would stay only in our hearts as captured on film? I had many questions stirring in my mind, probably because it was Trish and Kevin's last day here. I had no idea when I would see Trish again, and I didn't want her to leave so soon. Trish's visit made Dad decide to meet Maureen, and it was almost as if Trish was an angel; she appeared out of nowhere and forced our family to spend time together. But now, she was off and who knows what would happen next.

I discussed my feelings with Gord on the way to brunch. He said that we had no way of predicting the future, but to be content with what occurred this weekend and to enjoy the rest of Trish's visit. He knew me so well. It was obvious that I had a need to control situations and ensure everyone got along, which only caused me to worry too much. I knew I needed to take his advice, live in the present, and not worry about the future. So I decided to try just that.

They had just finished eating when we arrived at the restaurant. It felt strange to walk in and see Dad with his two, new daughters and their respective husbands. It was almost like a movie scene and as soon as Dad saw me, he jumped up and gave me a hug. I sensed that even though he was bonding with his daughters, he still needed to see a familiar face to ground him. He was radiant but seemed a little nervous. They spoke about last night's events and how Dad drove

Trish back to her hotel since she was too exhausted to stay at the bar any longer. Trish winked at me, and I knew exactly what she was thinking. Here was the man who had barely pondered the thought of even meeting his daughters, and look at him now. He spent a lot more time with Trish and Maureen than any of us, especially me, had expected he would. I never dreamt he would give them so much of his time. I was sure that if I counted the number of hours he had spent with them, it would have probably exceeded the amount of time I had spent with him in years. Although, I was not complaining in the least, as Dad's participation with our family this past weekend had meant the world to me.

We chatted and remarked to each other about how time had just flown by and that we really must do it again; it was the kind of conversation families all over Canada and the world have everyday. Before we knew it, it was time for Dad to say goodbye to Trish and Maureen. They stood up and hugged each other. I did the same to Maureen and commented on how beautiful she looked. She appreciated my making the effort to compliment her and kissed me on the cheek. Dad turned to me, gave me a hug goodbye, and said, "thank you" again. I thanked him back for the time he gave his daughters and for making them feel comfortable and welcomed into our family. I didn't know how much involvement he would have in their lives from this day forward, but I did know that they were an integral part of my life as well as Tina's, Lenny's and Rocky's, so he was sure to see them again. He now had four daughters and two sons in his life.

It is often very difficult for a father to appear emotional in front of a daughter who he wants to protect and guide, and Dad was no different. Sometimes it infuriated me that he would not open up and let me in, but as he stood there, I felt sorry for him. He had obviously carried a great deal of weight about with him for the last thirty plus years, and I wouldn't wish that on anyone. If anything, I think he was relieved that the secret was finally out.

Gord and I took Trish and Kevin downtown. We strolled around an area in Toronto called Yorkville. It was Sunday and not all the shops were open, so we mostly window shopped. Trish was flabbergasted at how expensive the merchandise was, at the few stores that we managed to go into and browse. I told her that this area was the most expensive in Toronto and that it would compare to London's finer districts. She laughed and said that she might shop here if she didn't have children. It was true, Gord and I spoiled ourselves since we didn't have children, but there was the remote possibility that I was pregnant, and wouldn't be able to shop my heart out in the near future.

After spending a few hours walking and having coffee, we headed back to the airport area. My family knew we would be at Tony Roma's at 3 p.m. for an early dinner, but I had no idea who would be showing up. I knew Dad wasn't, but Aunt Tina said she most likely would. I doubted my brothers would make it since they lived a fair distance away. When we walked into the restaurant, Tina was already waiting with Steve. Not long after that, Aunt Tina arrived, and we all had a wonderful dinner with great conversation. The mood was definitely a little somber since we didn't know when we were going to see Trish again; these last few moments were precious. I had every intention of going to England later on that year to meet my nieces and spend more time with Trish, but I had no idea when my other siblings would see her since they all had full time jobs and other financial obligations. Trish seemed happy that they would just keep in touch by phone or email.

I took a good look at Trish as she sat at the table and I tried to memorize each detail of her face, so that I could commit her face to memory. I had come this far, I wasn't going to let a single moment go by without relishing it.

Then, it was time for Gord and I to drive Kevin and Trish to the airport. Tina, Steve, and Aunt Tina said their goodbyes to Trish, and once again, I turned away as I knew my turn was coming all too soon.

In the car, Trish and Kevin thanked Gord and I for the entire weekend, and I could see Trish's eyes fill with tears. I wasn't any better, but I told her we would talk soon and that I hoped to see her later in the year in England. When we arrived at the airport, Kevin told Gord and I to just drop them off and not bother parking our car. It all happened so quickly, and I felt a little disappointed since I wanted to spend every last possible minute with Trish. But at least, we didn't have to have the long, drawn out goodbye. We just hugged, kissed, and said that we would miss each other but we would talk soon.

It seemed so quiet on the drive home; all I was aware of was the constant humming of the wheels on the road and the wind as it whistled past the windows. I wondered if every plane flying overhead was the one that carried Trish homeward and away from her new family. What was there left to do now? I felt as if there was a hole left in my life, not so much from her leaving, but from having found her. The journey to this point had been so challenging and so unyielding that I had let it take over my life, and now that it was over, I didn't know what would replace it.

It was in these quiet moments that I thought of Mom; sometimes with sadness, sometimes with joy, but always with the sense that she was beside me like some beautiful angel. I tapped the window and watched the road speed by. People were either going away or coming home and, to be honest, I was not sure which I preferred anymore. The last few years had taken its toll on both Gord and I, and the last thing I had ever imagined was to gain two sisters but lose a loved one.

11.
THE JOURNEY CONTINUES, THE TRAVELING BEGINS

It was Halloween night, and I had to hire a neighbor to hand out the candy since I had an evening flight to England. My husband stayed with me at the terminal right up until boarding time. I was very emotional at the thought of my journey. Every few minutes, I found myself taking a slow deep breath to control the tears of nervousness, excitement, and anticipation. This was my first flight alone; my first trip to Europe, and I was going to see Trish. I was also excited to be meeting my nieces for the first time. Gord wished me well and kissed me goodbye; through blurred vision, I watched him walk away.

I boarded the plane and was seated beside a very pleasant elderly couple. An uneasy excitement came over me as the plane ascended, and my heart began beating faster and faster. An overwhelming desire to cry was within me all the time, and I fought hard every second to blink back the tears and remain composed. October 31st was an interesting date for me: it was the eve of Mom's death, only eight short years ago, and the birthday of my beloved Memère Rose. And now, it was also the date of my first visit to Trish's home.

All over the globe people were celebrating Halloween; putting on costume, participating in rituals and symbolic acts designed to evoke or keep away evil spirits. There is something about this day, of all days perhaps, that connects us to our history. It represents the mingling of Christian and pre-Christian ideas about ancestry, and the continuum of life. For me, the symbols of All Soul's Eve are more personal; they are the tiny reminders of that which is gone, ghosts, if you like. However, I was adding more portents to this date and that was frightening in itself.

The elderly couple beside me was on their way to Scotland. We enjoyed our wine and spirits as we spoke throughout the flight. I couldn't believe the amount of brandy they were able to consume and yet still be coherent. The more they talked, the more they drank. The more I listened, the more they insisted I match them. Every time I tried to stop them, they just bought me more, one after the other; unfortunately, about an hour before landing, I realized that I had consumed too much. Suddenly, I felt dizzy and nauseous. I asked the flight attendant for some water and a blanket. With an hour left until touchdown, I felt embarrassed and hoped a little nap would sober me up.

I awoke to the captain announcing our descent to Manchester airport. I felt very groggy and quickly went to the washroom to freshen up. I looked a little pale, but my eyes weren't as red as I had anticipated. They were just baggy as they always were. Peering through the small window, I began feeling nervous again. Airports were intimidating at the best of times and now I was alone. Kevin, Trish's husband, was meeting me by himself. I was actually thankful now that Trish and the girls weren't with him since I didn't have the energy for all the excitement they would cause.

Still, I couldn't wait to meet them. I had developed a wonderful relationship with Trish since I first met her nine months ago. We called each other every couple of weeks, and my love for her grew each time we spoke. We were not only sisters, but great friends as well. We were both so excited about my visit to their home. Trish had a very busy agenda for us, and I was totally game. Since Trish and I were so alike, I knew that she would have spent a great deal of time arranging everything and hoping it would all go perfectly.

I got off the plane and felt the cold English air hit me as I walked down the steps. I was thankful for it, because it knocked the last of the brandy's fuzziness from me, and I was thinking, seeing and feeling clearly again.

After picking up my luggage, I went through the gates and spotted Kevin immediately. He smiled and gave me a big hug. It was 9 a.m. and I prayed that he didn't smell my alcohol-laced breath, but unfortunately, he did. And in his Yorkshire accent he said, "Debbie! You smell like you just came from a bar." I felt embarrassed and explained how an elderly Scottish couple was on a mission to get me drunk and they succeeded. He laughed and said that he shouldn't be nagging me since he was quite hung over himself from the late night he had.

THE JOURNEY CONTINUES, THE TRAVELLING BEGINS

We walked to his car, and I automatically went to sit in the driver's seat, which would have been the passenger's seat in Canada. The awkwardness of sitting opposite to what I was usually accustomed to intensified as he drove out of the parking lot; I yelled out at him because I instinctively thought he was driving on the wrong side of the road. This driving on the opposite side of the road was going to take getting used to, and I wasn't in the frame of mind to adjust quickly. It only added to my nausea, and I asked Kevin if he could drive nice and slow in the two-hour ride to their house. We spoke of many things and he pointed out various interesting landscapes. I was fascinated with all the lush greenery and rolling hills and understood what Kevin meant when he characterized Toronto as a "cement city." At least, the rain was good for something in England. In fact, it was raining as we drove and according to Kevin, the forecast for the rest of my visit was mostly rain.

As we neared their house, Kevin pointed out some local restaurants and pubs, a couple of small hotels and their place of work. Their home was situated in a small town called Pontefract. I noticed a lot of new development. We approached their house, which was nearly new, and I found it to be wonderfully charming. It seemed to have far too much character for a six-month-old house.

As we pulled into the driveway, Trish immediately came running out. She gave me a big hug and kiss and before she spoke, I apologized for not feeling the greatest from the lack of self-control on the plane. She laughed and said that I just proved the reason why she hardly ever drank anything on a plane. We went into the house through the back entrance and walked into the kitchen. It was so fresh and clean, and I couldn't wait to see the rest of the house. Trish took me from room to room and each one was so lovely and clean. When we entered Sally-Ann's room, where she said I would be sleeping, there was a beautiful bouquet of freshly cut flowers in a vase with a card attached. It read, "Welcome to our home." I nearly cried as I hugged Trish thank you and told her that she was so thoughtful.

Kevin brought my luggage upstairs, and we all went down to the kitchen for a cup of tea. As we chatted, they noticed how lousy I felt, so Trish suggested I have a nap while she ran some errands. She hoped that I would feel better before we went to pick up her girls. I appreciated her thoughtfulness and ran upstairs. As soon as my head hit the pillow, I felt nauseous and was furious with myself for being so stupid in drinking so much. I finally drifted off to sleep for about an hour, after which, Trish woke me and said that she was just about to pick up her daughters. So I jumped out of bed, eager to see my nieces.

I ran and hopped into the back seat of their car as the rain came pouring down. I stared at the rain as I had never seen rain come down so hard in my life; England was living up to its reputation. We first picked up Sally-Ann, who had just turned five. Kevin just honked for her seeing as it was raining so hard. As we waited, I rolled down the window in hopes of easing my nausea. I explained to Trish and Kevin that I was a lousy back seat passenger at the best of times, and how Tina and I were both often car sick when we were children. I kept apologizing, but Trish insisted I be quiet and not worry about anything. As I rolled the window back up, a little girl came running towards the car. She sat down beside me and said questioningly, "You're Debbie?"

I told her that she was correct and we hugged. She was so beautiful, and I couldn't take me eyes off hers. Her eyes were as gorgeous as in the first picture I ever saw of her; she looked a lot like Kevin to me. It was difficult to understand her since she spoke so quickly in her British accent, however, she was more comprehendible than the few times I had spoken with her over the phone. She held my hand as we went off to pick up her sister, Jennifer. Both Kevin and his mother thought Jenny looked so much like me, so I was looking forward to seeing if it was true. I knew we both had curly hair from the pictures I saw of her; I felt that there was a small resemblance, but now I was about to find out for certain. Trish ran into the childcare giver's house to get Jenny as Sally-Ann spoke non-stop to me.

When Trish returned, she placed Jenny in her car seat. I said hello to her, but she wouldn't speak. She just kept smiling and looking out the window in the opposite direction. She was obviously shy, and why wouldn't she be since I was a virtual stranger to this two year old. On our drive home, Jenny and I would take peeks at one another and I noticed that her profile definitely resembled me as a child. She was so cute with her big blue eyes and very curly locks. I caught her smiling, as she was playing coy with me.

Within an hour of being home with the girls, Jenny warmed up to me, and it was fun playing with my new nieces. The two of them had enough energy for five children, and I was disappointed that I was still tired after my journey and the drinks. We had a bite to eat for dinner, and I excused myself straight after that and changed into my pajamas. I purchased new "Nick & Nora" pajamas specifically for this trip, and I knew the girls would laugh at me when they saw them. When I came down the stairs looking like a leopard, both the girls, along with Trish and Kevin, laughed at me. It was around 6 p.m. when the phone rang. It was Kevin's parents wanting to come over and meet me. I understood their excitement since they were so close to Trish and were so happy for her to have met her birth family. However, I really wasn't up for the company and Trish told them as much. They wouldn't accept any excuses, so I told them it would be fine, but that I wasn't going to change out of my pajamas. They would just have to meet me in my "Jungle Jim" pj's.

Kevin's parents rang the doorbell at what seemed like just five minutes after they had called. It took every bit of strength in me to have any kind of composure, but I think I managed. Kevin's mum, Eileen, hugged me immediately, and I noticed how beautiful she was. Kevin's dad shook my hand and jokingly thanked me for dressing up for them. I laughed and knew I was going to have my hands full with this character. We only chatted for about an hour since we knew we'd see each other in a few days. Hopefully I'd be feeling more like myself then.

After Kevin's parents left, Trish somehow managed to talk me into getting dressed and going to a local pub. She made a good argument explaining that this was my first night here and she didn't want to waste any time getting to know her sister better. The pub looked like an authentic English pub, or at least what I had envisioned as typical. Trish and I sat by the fireplace. As we spoke, we noticed that the background music was soft and romantic and we both smiled and sang along. After one drink, I felt better and ordered another. It dawned on me how strange it was to be in England sitting across from my parents' first born child; my eldest sister. I shared my feelings with Trish and she recalled feeling the same way when she was in Toronto in January, meeting her huge birth family. If I was feeling the bizarre nature of these circumstances, I couldn't imagine how she felt being raised as an only child to then find out, only a year ago, that she had five siblings. I wished I could walk in her shoes for a while to experience the other side; I wondered what it was like to be the adoptee.

We spoke easily of many things for a couple of hours and then decided we better head home since the girls would wake early. I fell asleep at around midnight but was restless all night since I wasn't in my own bed. It felt strange to be in another country so far from my own. I felt as though I crossed over more than the ocean to get here. I felt as though I crossed over time and people's lives. Things were so different here and yet Trish had made me feel at home.

I awoke to little girls laughing and knocking on my door; they came into the room and greeted me with big smiles. They were so cute and so full of energy, something I was still lacking. I felt like I hadn't slept for very long, and my feeling was confirmed when I went down to the kitchen and noticed that the clock read 5:45 a.m. Trish wasn't exaggerating when she told me that the girls were early risers, and since the clocks had recently been set back an hour, the girls were up even earlier. I felt a little bleary eyed after my flight and lack of sleep, but I splashed some water on face and told myself to pull myself together. I was in England now; I had to enjoy every minute of it.

Trish and Kevin told me that they wanted to take me to York for a shopping day without the girls. The rain was still coming down, and the skies looked as grey as I had ever seen them. The radio and television stations warned of flooding in many regions of England and to take extreme caution when traveling by car. It was also very cold which made the dampness feel worse. We dropped the children off and proceeded to drive to York. The roads were horrible and some were actually closed due to the flooding, so Kevin wasn't sure if we would be able to make it, but we eventually reached our destination.

York was magnificent with its cobblestone walkways, exclusive shops, quaint restaurants serving afternoon tea and the historical York Minster Cathedral. We toured the Cathedral and experienced the majestic aura of it. I was absolutely speechless at the enormity and the beautiful details within the walls. It was like nothing I'd ever seen before. This was history dating all the way back to 1253.

I couldn't help but feel so insignificant and small in such an old and important building. Trish wanted to light a candle in honor of her mother and I followed suit. When I lit my candle, I had tears in my eyes as I thanked Mom for whatever hand she played in bringing my sisters and I together. I looked at Trish and noticed that she appeared quite emotional as well. I whispered in her ear that our mothers had probably met in heaven and could see us together at this very moment. It felt strange to me to say, "our mothers" when in fact we only truly had one mother; the same one who gave birth to both of us. However, I fully understood that to Trish, her only mother was the one she knew. I could hear in Trish's voice and see in her eyes how very much she loved her mother. It pleased me that she had such a close relationship with her. I silently thanked her mother for adopting my sister and giving her a wonderful life.

Mom would be so proud of her eldest daughter; for the beautiful woman she had become and for all of her accomplishments. I thought of Maureen's mother at this moment as well. It was unfortunate that Maureen hadn't received as much love from her adoptive mother as Trish and I had from our own mothers. Maureen had become her own wonderful woman, possibly due to her father, but mostly due to herself.

The candle flames flickered in the slight breeze of the Cathedral, each once dancing to its own tune, just like the spirits they represented. I just watched them for a moment; each one bright against the grey walls. I imagined how each one held a story, how each one represented a loved one gone, but a memory retained. The lucky ones are the loved ones who leave behind those who light candles in their honor. Each tiny flame here represented a tiny spark of love left behind and passed on; to see light coming from a hundred candles made me feel as though I wasn't alone, wherever I was in the world.

I didn't take too many pictures inside the Cathedral since I knew a picture couldn't capture its enormity or stunning details. However, I asked Kevin to take a picture of Trish and I sitting on a bench inside the Cathedral. I also purchased a booklet that included beautiful photographs and some history. Kevin and I went down into the archives that we both found fascinating.

After leaving York Minster, the three of us went shopping. Unfortunately, it was pouring with rain, and we had to run from shop to shop in order to stay dry. Trish bought herself a silver toothpick which I thought was a little unusual, but apparently she had wanted one for some time since she used them frequently. Trish and I spent quite some time in a leather shop trying on tight little mini skirts and leather pants. We wore the same size, but she was a few inches taller, which made her look more slender than me. We had tons of fun in the store, but to Kevin's surprise, left empty handed.

We decided to go for high tea at around 2 p.m. The rain wasn't pleasant but I wasn't going to let it ruin our day; I was loving every minute of this whole experience. We shopped a bit more before heading to a pub for a bite to eat and beer to warm us up. As we sat in the pub talking, and laughing, I realized how much I really liked Kevin; I found him quite amusing. Kevin and Trish made a great couple, and watching them interact made me think of Gord and I suddenly felt his absence.

We spent the evening at home and turned in early since Trish and I planned to wake up at 5 a.m. to catch a train to London. The weather channel indicated flooding in many regions, but didn't show any train cancellations. I went to bed concerned that our London trip might be cancelled since I really wanted to go shopping.

The next morning, it was still raining but thankfully, our train was scheduled to leave on time. We left the house at 6 a.m. and even though I felt tired, I was too excited to think about it. It was only raining slightly, but it was absolutely freezing cold. The dampness chilled me to the bone while waiting for our train. We were booked on an express train that would take us approximately two hours to get to London.

Fortunately, our train arrived on time and we found seats together. It was so cold on the train, and I couldn't imagine two hours of shivering, so we kept moving seats until we found a warmer area. Less fortunate though, was our journey itself, as the train stopped every half an hour for an hour, and we ended up taking five cold and frustrating hours to reach London. Trish was absolutely annoyed and called Kevin to complain. He suggested we get a room in London and stay overnight since our day was already shortened. I completely agreed with Kevin. I thought it would be fun, but Trish said we'd play it by ear; we didn't bring any toiletries, although I was sure we could manage.

We finally arrived in London at midday and took a local train to our first destination, Buckingham Palace. We were standing on the train and Trish noticed a piece of gum on the floor and pointed it out to me. The train was very crowded with all walks of life and outrageous styles that I enjoyed observing, but Trish and I seemed more fixated on this piece of gum, wondering who would step on it. We watched as different feet came close to stepping on it. All of a sudden, we couldn't stop giggling; we were delirious with laughter and tears were streaming down our faces.

It was one of those moments where you are so exhausted that you become delirious enough to release the emotion with laughter. A few people were staring at us, but we didn't care. Finally, someone stepped on the gum and we started howling with laughter. It was our stop to get off, and we pushed our way out of the train. We started to calm down as we walked, in the cold but sunny day, to Buckingham Palace.

I noticed the unbelievably beautiful buildings on the way, and Trish mentioned that they were extremely expensive flats.

We finally reached Buckingham Palace, but I was disappointed that I couldn't get close enough to see the guards. I wanted pictures of Trish in front of the gate and that's when a man motioned to us that he would take a picture of the two of us. When I handed him my camera, I couldn't help but notice how handsome he was. He was even better looking than any movie star on film. Trish and I stood in front of the gate, and we were commenting on how he was an eleven out of ten on the looks scale as we smiled for the picture. I thanked him and when he replied, "You're welcome," I noticed his French accent, which made him even sexier. We walked to a nearby sandwich shop where we talked a little more about the tall, dark, handsome stranger over tea and a sandwich. Trish wanted me to see Big Ben and a couple of other attractions nearby, but we didn't have our own vehicle and there was no tour bus to catch, and it was too cold to walk. I told her that I would be just as happy to go shopping.

And shopping we did! We went to Harrods, the world renowned department store, where I purchased some Christmas decorations and viewed the breathtaking window displays. We then made our way to Covent Garden where we spent the rest of the day going from shop to shop. I purchased a pair of fabulous boots at L. K. Bennett, and I couldn't wait to show them off back home. Prices were expensive, but everything was so modern that I knew I'd get at least a few seasons out of them.

With our bags weighing us down, we realized how famished we were and decided to dine at a posh French restaurant. The atmosphere was elegant, and we really enjoyed talking over exquisite wine and a delicious meal. Trish decided that we should travel back home instead of grabbing a hotel room, and I have to admit I was a little disappointed. I really would have enjoyed more alone time with Trish, but I didn't say anything.

We shopped a little more and then went for a coffee and dessert before starting our journey home. It was a warm, trendy little café; we sat in comfy armchairs, so we could take our shoes off and curl up. The day in London was ending and I didn't want it to.

The train was due to leave at 8 p.m. and was expected to arrive back in York at 10:30 p.m., but it didn't depart until 9 p.m. so we were half an hour late even before we left the station! We were both exhausted but still exhilarated by our day together in London. We spoke of our purchases and the dream man in front of Buckingham Palace. Trish dozed off, and I began speaking with a gentleman who was seated beside us. I told him about my reasons for visiting England and about meeting Trish and Maureen. He was fascinated and listened to every word I said. I told him about Trish, and her trip to Canada, and how this was my first time in the UK.

Talking to him, I realized how fantastic my story seemed. I loved to tell people my story and see how they reacted. After our conversation, I stared out of the window at the blackness that engulfed the train, and I drifted off to sleep. When I woke up, we were almost home, but it was a little after 1 a.m. which meant that the train had stopped again during our trip. Trish was now speaking with the man I had talked to earlier; she was telling him how annoyed she was with this entire train experience, and how we had basically been on the train for ten long hours when it should have been only four or five hours.

Trish found a comment card and filled it out. She let them know that she found the system incompetent and wanted her tickets reimbursed. She signed her name with "Doctor" in the hopes that they would take her comments more seriously. There were many times when I looked at Trish and thought that she reminded me of myself. Particularly in her mannerisms and how stubborn she could be at times. Now I knew how my husband sometimes felt. All I could think of was that we should have stayed overnight in London like Kevin had suggested. Trish was acting exactly how I did when I had my mind set on something, and it was amusing to watch a double of myself in action. We were definitely sisters!

We reached the train station at 1:30 a.m. and drove home. It was 2 a.m. when we finally hit the pillows. All I could think of was that the girls would be waking me up in a few short hours.

It seemed like only a few hours, but it was actually 8 a.m. when I woke up. Six whole hours, but I was still feeling totally spent. I went downstairs, and the girls gave me a hug. Children truly have a knack for making you feel special, and it was times like these that I felt the absence of a child in my life. I thanked Kevin for keeping the girls out of my room that morning, allowing me a couple of extra hours of sleep.

It was Saturday morning, and our plans were to visit Kevin's parents at their house and meet his entire family, including six of his nieces and nephews. I was still feeling very tired and looked worse, but

I wanted to meet them since Kevin was such a nice person; besides, if they were anything like him, it would be a lot of fun.

As soon as we walked into Kevin's parents' house, I noticed how loud it was with all the children playing. I met two of Kevin's brothers and his sister, and they were lovely people. Kevin's father, being the joker he was, told me that I had aged ten years since he saw me last. I knew the bags under my eyes were bad, but now I felt subconscious and just wanted to go home to sleep. However, Kevin's father announced we were all going to a pub later that night to have a few drinks together. I was just too exhausted to go out, so I told Trish that I would probably stay in.

Trish went out and picked up authentic fish and chips for dinner which I was looking forward to having. My plans were to stay home and watch the girls, but after I ate the heavy meal I felt more energetic and decided to join the gang at the pub. After all, it was my second to last night in England, and I wanted to experience as much as I could.

We spent the night laughing and drinking in the busy and crowded atmosphere of the pub. Kevin's Dad kept buying me pints, and after about three, I had forgotten how tired I was and started chatting about anything and everything. The faster I drank, the faster he bought them for me. I felt drunk, for almost the third time in as many days. They closed the place down at the early hour of 11 p.m. I was surprised that the pubs closed so early in England or at least, in Yorkshire.

We headed back to Trish's home. Once Kevin's parents and sister left, Kevin, Trish and I sat up talking until almost 2 a.m. I was still exhausted, but my time was so limited with Trish that I wanted to make the most of it.

I woke up at 7 a.m. the next morning and realized it was Sunday, my last full day with them. We stayed home for most of the day, but we went grocery shopping so I could buy lots of chocolate to bring home. The Cadbury's chocolate in England was the best in the world, and I wanted to bring lots home with me. We also went to a local candy shop where I purchased Thornton's toffee as it came highly recommended.

We arrived home, and Trish prepared a proper English prime rib dinner with all the trimmings. Our dinner was fantastic and after cleaning up, we all sat in the family room looking out the window at the fireworks lighting the sky for Robbie Burns Day. The girls turned in at 9 p.m., and I felt sad saying goodnight to them since this was our last night together for who knew how long. Even though they woke me early every morning, I was going to miss them; their abundance of energy, and their affectionate nature. Kevin went to bed at 10 p.m. leaving Trish and I alone to talk a little. I thanked her for everything and mostly for making me feel like part of their family. She looked as exhausted as I did, so we decided to turn in early since we had to leave the house at 7:30 a.m. to go to the airport. Kevin's mum, Eileen, would be joining us as well.

The next morning arrived quickly, and I woke early to pack my suitcases. I had arranged most things the night before, so it didn't take me too long to pack everything neatly in the luggage. Kevin helped the girls get ready since it was Monday morning. I kissed the three of them goodbye. As I thanked Kevin for his wonderful hospitality, I started feeling emotional again, so I asked him to take the girls and hurry off.

Trish and I loaded my luggage into the back of her car, and I realized that my luggage definitely weighed more this time. I smiled as I wondered aloud to Trish if the weight had anything to do with all the sweets? We picked up Eileen, and made our way through the horrendous rain to the airport. The weather was miserable throughout my entire stay -according to the news forecasters, England had a record rainfall - but I still had a fabulous time. Trish and Eileen came into the airport with me, and we had coffee and Danish. As I was eating, my throat tightened, and I thought I was going to breakdown at any moment. I told them they had better get going since I couldn't handle a prolonged goodbye. I started crying on our way to the security gate and all at once, I stopped to hug Trish. I attempted to tell her thank you, but my speech was impaired since I was bawling so hard. Trish had tears rolling down her cheeks, but she could at least speak. She thanked me for making the journey and wished me a safe flight home. All I could do was nod. I quickly hugged Eileen goodbye before passing security. We waved to each other when I was through.

Once they were out of sight, I took a deep breath and told myself to get a grip and stop acting like a child. I figured my exhaustion made me even more emotional than I would have been. I had an hour and a half to kill before boarding the plane, so I wandered around the shops and decided to sit and have one last pint of beer. It felt good to relax and think about my time in England. The weather had been lousy, but I met my beautiful little nieces, Kevin's awesome family and most importantly, I bonded further with Trish. Now I had a seven-hour plane ride home and I was looking forward to seeing my wonderful husband.

I felt as though I had experienced something more than meeting my sister in England. I felt as if I had united my family again. Somehow, even though we had only known each other for a short while, I felt as if I had known Trish my entire life. I felt as though she was waiting to be found by me. Perhaps all things - books, songs, poems, loved ones - are just waiting to be found by the right person, who just happens to come along. Perhaps some are never found and spend their whole lives not knowing who they are, or who they belong to. I knew as I left Trish at the airport that more than anything, I belonged to her as she belonged to me, and to the rest of my family.

I sat in my airplane seat with the early morning light shining in my eyes. I gazed out of the small window, past the wet tarmac, up at the English sky that was watching over Trish, my sister.

SISTERS REVEALED

12.
COMING HOME

Gord was waiting for me at the airport, and as soon as I saw him I became emotional again. I kissed and hugged him and realized at that moment how much I missed him. I had been too busy in England to think about him that often, but now, I couldn't wait to get home to our bed and have a good night's sleep. The only problem was that it was early afternoon, Toronto time, so I would only be able to have a short nap as I didn't want to mess up my sleeping pattern.

Once I woke from my nap, I showed Gord my new boots, and he agreed that they were exquisite. After unpacking, we shared a bottle of wine while I told him all about my five days in England. He wasn't surprised that Trish and I related so well since he felt that we had similar personalities. I gave him the rolls of film I took, and he said that he would drop them off later that day and pick them up tomorrow. It would be so much easier to describe some of my outings with pictures.

I went to bed a happy girl that night. I was in the comfort of my own bed with my man beside me. I felt totally complete. My family was whole and I got along well with both my long lost sisters. I realized I had more in common with Trish, but I loved them both equally.

The next morning, I awoke feeling a little lonely. Gord had left for work, which wasn't unusual, but the house felt so empty. It seemed so quiet. Normally, I appreciated the peace, but that day I felt so alone and isolated. I called Trish at work to let her know I had arrived safely, but I received her voicemail instead, so I left a message. I realized that I actually missed the sound of chaos within the walls of Trish's home; sounds of children's laughter and parents always chatting to children. The utter silence in my home left me wanting a child.

I had been unsuccessful thus far with the fertility clinic and was scheduled for a laparoscopy on December 1st to determine if there were any physical reasons for my lack of success in conceiving. I hoped that this minor surgery would prove to be successful. Both Trish and Maureen wanted me to get pregnant; Maureen went as far as to offer to be a surrogate mother. I really appreciated her offer even if she wasn't completely serious. I told her that at this point there was still no reason why I shouldn't be able to conceive.

I had grown used to the sound of a busy family around me. In a strange way, I missed being woken up far too early by the smiling faces of children who would make me feel awake and alive as soon as they hugged and kissed me. I missed having them around to cheer me up and not give me a moment's peace. I missed their constant questions and their smiles, but most of all I missed the way they made me feel as though I would never be alone again.

December 1st approached quickly and Gord drove me to the hospital at 7 a.m. He was surprised by how calm I seemed, but this wasn't the first time I was given general anesthesia for a medical procedure. At this point, I wanted results and reasons as to why I wasn't getting pregnant. I kissed Gord before going to the operating room, and he said he'd see me in an hour.

I awoke to Gord sitting beside me. He kissed my forehead and asked how I was feeling. Before I had the chance to respond, the doctor appeared. As soon as I saw the expression on the doctor's face, I knew he was about to give me bad news. He explained to me that I had moderate endometriosis and that he had removed some on my ovaries. He said that this condition was probably the reason for my inability to conceive with the method I was trying. He wouldn't go into the details and asked to make an appointment to see him in a couple of weeks to go over my options. When the doctor left, I looked at Gord and my eyes filled with tears. I didn't cry but I was very emotional and the general anesthesia didn't help. I just wanted to get out of the hospital and be home. Once at home, Gord tucked me in, on the couch, and went to the pharmacy to fill my pain prescription.

As I lay alone with my thoughts, I became angry. *Why did I have to have endometriosis? What was wrong with me?* I was feeling sorry for myself since I had three sisters who all conceived without difficulties. All I could think of was, "Why me?" Then I wondered what the doctor had meant by options; at least I had options.

I spoke with my three sisters about my problem, and they all tried to comfort me. In fact, Trish mentioned that she had endometriosis, which I had no idea about, and she still conceived two children. Both

Trish and Maureen were very sympathetic, and once again Maureen brought up the subject of her being a surrogate for me. Tina was fully aware of the condition since her sister-in-law, Pam, had an extreme case of it and had been trying to get pregnant for years.

I went back to the couch after speaking with everyone. I still felt some self-pity but also immense joy for having two more sisters to share my feelings with. I also felt fortunate that, even if I couldn't have my own children, at least I had a large family with nieces that I could have close relationships with. Gord was sitting in a chair across from me, and he looked sad. He never really expressed to me the extent of his disappointment at not conceiving, but I could see it in his eyes. It took Gord a long time to want a child, and now, there were all these obstacles in our way. We both sat in silence, pondering this new block in the road.

The phone rang, breaking the uneasy silence between Gord and I. As Gord answered the phone, I said I wasn't in the mood to talk to anyone just yet. I heard him say hello and then he handed me the phone saying that I might want to take this call. It was my cousin Lisa, Aunt Linda's daughter, who had rarely if ever called us.

Lisa called to inform me that Memère Rose had been taken to Belleville Hospital and that the prognosis was not good. Aunt Linda had already left for the hospital. She had asked Lisa to call me, knowing how close I was to Memère Rose. I told Lisa that I just had minor surgery and couldn't go anywhere. I told her that I would call the hospital to find out what was going on and thanked her for the call.

I didn't cry when I was on the phone with Lisa, but as soon as I hung up, I cried. "Not Memère Rose," was all I could say to Gord. She couldn't die on me; I considered Memère Rose as my second mother, and I needed her. I felt so sick, and my heart ached. Gord gave me another painkiller, and I told him I wanted to go to the hospital. He absolutely refused to drive me in my condition, especially since it was a good two hours away. However, he did call the hospital for me. A nurse at the hospital informed me that Memère Rose was in a stable condition but had undergone a traumatic incident and that they weren't quite sure what steps to take yet. It was likely that Memère Rose would need to be transferred to Kingston Hospital's cardiac care unit. All this information was scaring me, and I asked her if Memère Rose had a heart attack. The nurse explained that it was heart failure where her heart rate had gone down to 10 beats per minute before being resuscitated. I hung the phone up and cried even harder. Gord reminded me of the fact that Memère Rose was still alive and that if anyone could make it through this, it was my grandmother; she was the strongest woman we knew.

The painkiller was taking its effect, and I finally drifted into a fitful sleep. I thought about Memère Rose as I drifted off, and I remembered her telling me that she was so happy to have had the opportunity to meet Trish and Maureen before she died. It could be all over for her now but I took comfort in knowing that her lifelong wish had been fulfilled.

I called Belleville Hospital the next day, and they informed me that Memère Rose had been rushed to Kingston Hospital because her heart had failed again. And once again, they had managed to revive her. I called Kingston Hospital, and they reassured me that Memère Rose was in a stable condition but was extremely confused and scared. The nurse said she required a pacemaker but that she would be okay providing her heart didn't fail in the interim. I felt better physically but very emotionally drained. I called Tina, Lenny and Rocky, and we all agreed to travel together the next day to Kingston. Memère Rose was an important woman in all our lives, and we wanted to give her our love and encouragement.

It was very sad to see her in the hospital but other than the black bruises on her chest, she looked well. Memère Rose was crying and telling us how scared she was to wake up in the hospital not knowing what had happened. We went in the room, two at a time, and agreed that this lady was a survivor. She was very lucky that all she needed was a pacemaker. It was already in her body, and she said she couldn't even feel it. We all stayed for a bit and then said our goodbyes, knowing Memère Rose was going to be fine. She thanked us repeatedly for coming to see her. She said that we were just like her own children and that she loved us very much.

As I left the hospital, I could not help but be reminded of the time I had visited Mom; I felt that I could not bear to go through it with Memère Rose as well.

When I arrived home, I called Trish and Maureen to let them know what had happened to Memère Rose. They were both relieved that she made it through okay. Their relationship with her was just beginning, and Trish wanted her daughters to have the opportunity to meet their great-grandmother. It was yet another episode that confirmed how precious life was; if there is something you badly wanted to do, there's no point in waiting to do it.

Gord and I had an appointment to meet the fertility doctor a week before the Christmas holidays. It was driving me crazy imagining what options he was talking about, so I kept myself busy with Christmas shopping. Tina and Steve were having Christmas at their house this year, which meant Maureen and Megan would be spending their first Christmas with our family. It was too bad that Trish and her family couldn't be with us as well, but I knew it was an unrealistic wish.

Gord and I were waiting anxiously in the doctor's office for our name to be called. I felt nervous and afraid, but Gord was optimistic that everything would be okay. He was the eternal optimist and, of course, I was the pessimist. We always joked about our differences, but felt we balanced one another out. The doctor called my name, and we followed him into his big, cozy office. He first showed us a diagram of my reproductive organs, and where the endometriosis had implanted itself, and then he explained the procedure we had undertaken the week before. He went on to explain my two options. The first being a hormone therapy program that would stop my menstrual cycle for five months by putting my body into a false menopause, and hopefully prevent further endometriosis from growing. The second option was in-vitro fertilization.

He gave us a brochure to take home and quickly explained what the procedure was for in-vitro. It involved hormone drugs, lots of needles and of course lots of money, but he indicated that it had the best success rate. I asked him which option he recommended and he said that he sat on the fence since they both had about a 50% chance, but if time was an issue, then in-vitro could make it happen quicker. We thanked the doctor for his time and said that we would make our decision soon.

Gord and I went for lunch and discussed our options further. Actually, there wasn't much to discuss since I was totally against the hormone therapy treatment. Gord said that it was my body, and he would support any decision I made, so we made a toast to trying in-vitro in the New Year.

Like always, Christmas was a time when our family came together. This year was made all the more special because we celebrated it at Tina and Steve's house with Maureen, Paul and Megan.

We phoned Trish, and we all individually wished her a Merry Christmas. It was already very late in England, but Trish sounded happy and wished that she was with us. It was during family moments like these that I really missed Mom. I only hoped that she could see us all together enjoying her favorite holiday. Dad showed up after dinner and didn't stay long, but at least he made an appearance and wished us all a Merry Christmas. Surprisingly, he didn't seem nervous around Maureen even though he hadn't seen or spoken to her since their first meeting almost a year ago. He enjoyed playing with his granddaughter Megan, and she started calling him "Little Grampa" just like Tina's daughter Shanelle did.

I found it interesting to see how Shanelle and Megan interacted considering that they were five years apart in age, and up until two years ago, Shanelle was the only grandchild. Megan was three going on four, and Shanelle treated her like the sibling she always wanted. They got along beautifully and Megan adored her new, older cousin. Tina had told Shanelle about her cousins in England when they met Trish earlier in the year. It was unfortunate that Trish didn't live nearby because Shanelle seemed to enjoy having cousins. It must have been strange for Shanelle to suddenly have cousins in her life. She was only eight, but she seemed to understand the situation and welcomed the new additions to our family.

Memère Rose was soon out of hospital and got stronger and stronger everyday. We sometimes joked that she was so strong that she would outlast us all, and sometimes, I thought that it might actually happen.

Day one of my cycle fell on the 1st of January, 2001. I was supposed to call the fertility clinic to let them know that I wanted to proceed with the in-vitro, but their office was closed. I had to wait a couple of days until they re-opened. The number I was given was for a girl named Beth, who apparently was the co-coordinator. I reached her voicemail and left a message. It didn't really matter because in all likelihood I would be declined this month, especially since they were closed down for a two week holiday. I was informed that it may even take three months to get accepted. I didn't receive a call back until the next day, when I was at work. My phone rang, and it was Beth. She said, "Okay, you're in." I had to ask her if that meant I was accepted that month, and she said "Yes." Then, she told me to call someone else at their office who would go through my schedule with me, and show me how to self-administer the needles.

I hung up the phone quickly and ran to Gord's desk to give him a big hug. We were now only about six weeks away from having our babies implanted in me. As scared as I was about the whole thing, I couldn't contain my happiness about the possible outcome. Gord and I decided to only tell my best friend, Jen and not our families. I felt that as long as I had my husband and best friend by my side while I was going through the treatment, I would be fine.

With all the effort I had put into finding my sisters, it felt strange embarking on a journey to add to the family with a child of my own. I guess, perhaps, the energy I spent on bringing my family together could also be spent on creating a new life but, really, that was in the hands of the doctors and fate. I wasn't sure if I wanted to start on this journey, because I knew that it could be hard and lonely. However, I suppose something drives you on; some innate feeling makes you want to try, because hope is the only thing that keeps you going, even if it is the hardest thing in the world to maintain.

The next six weeks were chaotic to say the least. The needles weren't pleasant, but I kept my chin up and was extremely positive about the entire procedure. I had a number of eggs removed and fertilized before they implanted two embryos. The only thing they said I could do now was wait, and so I waited. Almost immediately I felt pregnant, and my spirits were uplifted. However, I realized that the mind is a powerful tool and perhaps I was only making my body think I was pregnant.

A couple of days before I was scheduled to have my pregnancy test, my world was shattered. I started my period and to say I was devastated is an understatement. When I told Gord, I could see the hurt in his eyes, but he stayed strong for me. I cried for what seemed like hours. The world did not seem fair. I so desperately wanted a child of my own; I only wanted to be able to do what everyone else did so easily.

I called Beth on Monday morning, and she informed me that there was still a slight chance that I might be pregnant; therefore, I still had to be tested. I hated having to face the clinic and to get a blood test that would only reveal what I already knew. I tried not to look at any of the staff, but Beth caught me on the way out. As soon as she said, "I'm sorry," I ran out of the office in tears. I couldn't even talk to her. On my drive home, I could barely see through my tears. The last time I felt a loss like this, was when Mom died.

There were so many emotions going through my head that I could barely think straight. When I arrived home I felt like yelling, but instead I started thinking about all the good things I had gained in my life. I had two new sisters and three new nieces. Even with these positive thoughts, I couldn't help but feel envious of my three sisters. *Why didn't they have difficulty conceiving children?* I was continually coming back to the "why me?" question. I knew that self-pity was a useless emotion that just served to make me feel worse, but I couldn't help it.

The phone rang at around noon, and it was Beth confirming that my pregnancy test was negative. She said that there was a reading which meant that at some point, I was pregnant but unfortunately, it hadn't lasted. I was glad to hear this since it validated my feelings of being pregnant; it hadn't been just my imagination after all. I asked her when I could have the frozen embryo transfer, and she said I had to wait one full cycle and to call her on my next first day. I then told Beth that I heard some women talking in the waiting room about altering your immune system in case your system is too strong and would not accept the implants. She knew what I was referring to and said she'd talk to the doctor about whether or not he thought I was an eligible candidate.

I knew deep down, however, that this treatment was as much about luck, as it was about how your body reacted to situations. I tried to focus on the good things that had happened to me lately, but it was difficult. These procedures seemed to give so much hope and then just as easily, they could dash it all away, leaving you feeling empty and alone. I began, in some ways, to wish I had never started; after all, if you do not start, you will not get disappointed. Perhaps that was just my pessimism speaking; perhaps time would change my mind and prove me wrong.

I decided to tell my sisters about the failed attempts. They were all very surprised that I had kept it to myself since I usually divulged everything. Tina was especially shocked since she had seen me during my fertility treatment. She said she would never have guessed since I didn't seem different at all. They were all upset to hear that it didn't succeed, and they offered their comfort and support. I knew it was difficult for them; they couldn't understand why it wasn't working, and they couldn't relate to my position since they had children already. I knew they felt somewhat helpless, but they were there for me and it was enough.

Trish knew what would cheer me up; she announced that their family was coming to visit for two whole weeks in August in the upcoming summer. We had discussed this possibility earlier in the year, but I didn't think she was actually serious about it. I was thrilled, and I told her that I would help with the agenda and rent a cottage up north for a week. At least now, I had something to look forward to this summer!

I spent the next few months furiously planning for Trish's visit. It was quite a long way away, but I began early so everything would be perfect for their first visit as a whole family. This would be the first time Trish's daughters would be meeting their aunts, uncles, grandfather, cousins, and hopefully, great grandmother. Sally-Ann was nearly six years old and Jenny would actually be celebrating her third birthday during their visit on August 21st.

I told my father that they were coming and he expressed his interest in seeing his daughters again, and meeting his granddaughters from England. During conversations with Trish, she always referred to Dad as Rocky Senior. She intended to introduce him to her daughters as such, since she felt that they were too young to understand the nature of his presence in their mum's life. They already had two granddads, one in Ireland, and another in England, so Trish didn't want to confuse them. However, Trish did tell them that they had aunts and uncles and two cousins in Canada who wanted to meet them. Sally-Ann was so excited to meet Shanelle; when I had spoken to her recently on the phone, all she spoke about was coming to Canada and meeting Shanelle.

I searched for a great hotel for them to stay in for the first week, and I rented a cottage up north in Muskoka for the second week. The hotel was centrally located to all of my family, and when I checked it out, I felt sure that Trish's family would find it spacious and accommodating. Trish and I spent a lot of time on the phone in the two weeks prior to their departure.

I planned a very active first week, but the second week at the cottage would be more relaxing. After going through the agenda with Trish, she thanked me for helping to organize things. It would have been a difficult task for Trish to arrange everything from overseas. She had done the same thing for me when I visited England, which had helped me tremendously. I was so excited that they were spending their holidays with us.

I felt privileged that I didn't work full time, especially considering the last couple of years of meeting my sisters and also trying to get pregnant. My life truly felt like a roller coaster ride; all the heartache with the failure to conceive, and all the joy of meeting two beautiful sisters.

Now that Trish and her family were arriving for two whole weeks, not only did it mean that we'd be bonding with them, but it also meant that my entire family would be spending quality time together. Again, I felt bad for Maureen, because it appeared as though we went out of our way for Trish, but not for her. Maureen never said anything, but I wouldn't blame her if she felt that way, since I probably would myself if I were in her shoes. With this on my mind, I decided to give Maureen a call.

During my conversation with Maureen she never mentioned our over attentiveness towards Trish, but I decided to explain to her that it was exciting for us to have our English family come to visit. I also said that it would be a mini-vacation for our entire family and added that Trish's family were missing out on spending birthdays, Christmases and other holidays with us, so it would be a chance to make up for lost time. Maureen didn't argue with anything I said. She was most likely wondering why I even brought it up, but after speaking with her, I felt better knowing she understood. It was another prime example of me acting like Mom and ensuring nobody's feelings were hurt.

I always tried to include Maureen in whatever was going on. I appreciated that she was shy and sometimes might feel as if Trish took centre stage, but this was far from the truth. The truth is, I feel for Maureen more than she could ever know or I could ever explain.

The months passed by quickly. I tried my best to put my disappointments behind me and, because of all the planning I was doing, it became easier and easier. I made arrangements, organized hotels, made bookings, ensured that vehicles were hired and that everything was in place. I was determined that nothing was going to go wrong with Trish's visit and that she would come to know true Canadian hospitality.

13.
THE BIG VISIT

It was the night before Trish's arrival, and Gord and I sat in the family room discussing the agenda for the next two weeks. We were very busy at work in the summer months, which meant he wouldn't be able to join us for most of the events. It also meant that I had to spend a couple days a week at the office, during both weeks, but it fit into the schedule without any foreseeable problems. Gord looked at me wearing a big smile and said that I was going to be a very busy and tired girl in the next couple of weeks. He thought this was funny since I had been living a life of a semi-retired person without children and had been complaining of how bored I was at times. And now I was going to have my hands full. The excitement of having our entire family together, greatly outweighed any possible negative aspects of the upcoming weeks.

Surprisingly, my emotions were not acting up even though it was the day Trish's family was arriving. The first thing I had to do was go early to pick up the rental car, so Gord drove me to the shop. Typical of car rental places, they didn't have the car I had reserved. However, it turned out in my favor since I received a Taurus station wagon which was larger than the one I reserved, and they didn't charge me extra. Things were going well already. I drove back to Aurora and picked up some helium balloons with jellybeans in a bag for weights. I wanted to have something for the girls when they walked through the arrival gates. I would be alone at the airport this time, but Tina indicated that she would meet us at their hotel room after leaving work, which was only five minutes away from the hotel.

Their plane was scheduled to arrive at 1:30 p.m., so I arrived at the terminal at 1 p.m. Everyone was looking at me because I had balloons in my hand. The monitor showed that the flight was delayed for half an hour. It was no big deal; it just meant an extra half hour of people staring at me. I kept looking up at the flight board, and it kept saying that there were delays. Meanwhile, I was attracting more and more attention with my handful of balloons.

I was thinking about how exciting this was when I looked up and saw Gord. He laughed at my balloons and said that I certainly wasn't difficult to spot. He gave me a quick kiss, and I thanked him for coming and waiting with me.

The monitor indicated that their plane had landed, so we stood where the passengers walked into arrivals. Suddenly, my emotions came back into play, and I had to hold back tears. Sometimes, I felt as though the happy times made me cry more than the sad ones. Knowing how excited the girls were to be coming to Canada, I expected to hear Trish and her family before actually being able to see them. It dawned on me that Canada was the place their mother was born, which made it even more significant. I suddenly had the feeling that things were falling into place again, and that the family was becoming one again. I only wished that Mom was here to witness this moment with me. I'm sure she would have had a smile on her face and a balloon in her hand.

Just as I predicted, they were easy to spot. The girls had big smiles on their faces as they came around the corner. They came running towards me with big hugs and kisses as soon as they saw me. I gave them the balloons and jellybeans and as Sally-Ann was thanking me, she noticed Gord and said questioningly, "Uncle Gord?" He bent down and hugged her and said how nice it was to meet her. Then Jenny darted into his arms. I called Jenny "curly" and every time I saw her, she reminded me so much of myself.

I gave Trish and Kevin a big hug and a kiss after greeting the girls. Trish looked great and I told her as much. Gord greeted them, and they were both surprised and pleased to see him. We walked along the terminal to leave, when suddenly we heard a noise and saw Jenny's jellybeans scatter all over the floor. The bag had burst, and the jellybeans were everywhere. I don't know why, but Trish and I giggled as we tried to pick some up, but it was impossible to get them all. I could tell it was going to be quite the two weeks.

As we were leaving the terminal, Gord said he would pick me up from the hotel around 7 p.m. since I would need a ride home. Trish and Kevin liked the car, but I drove to the hotel since it was difficult to get out of the airport, never mind when you're from a country that drives on the opposite side of the road. I figured Kevin could practice once we were at the hotel.

THE BIG VISIT

When we reached the hotel the girls went running into the lobby. Everyone stopped to look at them and commented on how cute their British accents were. Kevin and Trish were very impressed with the room and felt that they would be comfortable during their stay. Trish commented that you would never find hotel rooms in Europe as big as this, unless you were willing to pay an exorbitant amount. The girls were excited that they each had their own bed.

Trish and I spoke as she unpacked an abundance of sweets that we started eating immediately. Later, we went for a quick bite at a family restaurant near the hotel. The girls spoke non-stop while we ate our meals; I had forgotten just how much energy they had. I was feeling tired already, and I thought that I had better start preparing myself for the coming two weeks.

As I watched Trish's family together, I thought what a great unit they made; each with their own separate personalities, but also with shared traits and characters. What one lacked, the others made up for; if one was tired, then the others would buoy them up; if one was shy, then another would be outgoing. I just loved to watch them being together, as a family and as they were.

We headed back to the hotel, and I was so filled with anticipation for witnessing Tina's first meeting with her nieces. Tina knew that Sally-Ann was excited to meet Shanelle, but unfortunately Shanelle was with her dad for the weekend; since their divorce, Tina and her husband had alternated weekends with their daughter. However, as we said to them, there was plenty of time for all the girls to get acquainted.

As we sat in the hotel room, there was a knock on the door and the girls went running to open it. Tina was standing there with her arms wide open to hug and kiss them both. She had only ever seen pictures and heard about Sally-Ann and Jenny from Trish and myself; now, she could experience them herself. She told them how beautiful they were, and they thanked her. Tina then gave Trish a big hug. I felt sorry for Kevin since he was always the last one to be acknowledged. Tina stayed for a little while and then Gord came to pick me up.

It was the 10th of August that Saturday, which meant it was Tina's 36th birthday. I had ordered a cake from the restaurant that we were due to celebrate in. Gord and I arrived at the Old Country Inn Restaurant early, to ensure that our table was set properly. Tina and Steve arrived shortly after us, followed by Rocky, Lenny and his girlfriend, Pip. We were scheduled to meet at 6 p.m. and it was around 6:30 p.m. already. I started getting nervous because Maureen and Trish's families had not yet arrived. Paul wasn't very good with directions, and Trish and Kevin were obviously relying on Paul and Maureen. Once 6:45 p.m. rolled by, I began panicking and stood in front of the restaurant just in case they missed the sign. Gord suggested I sit and relax since I had a tendency to overreact, but I continued to stand at the front of the restaurant. At 7 p.m., I spotted their vehicle and flagged them over. They parked and explained that they had left the hotel late because Paul had taken a nap in the afternoon since he wasn't feeling well.

Dinner was nice and when Tina's cake arrived at the table, we all sang "Happy Birthday." Afterwards, Trish invited everyone back to her hotel. I had a lot to prepare for the party we were having the next day - I was expecting up to twenty people – so, I had to decline her invitation and head home with Gord.

It was Sunday morning, and I picked up the rest of the food I had ordered. I was expecting people to start arriving around 2 p.m. Tina and Shanelle were the first ones. Shanelle was very excited to be finally meeting her cousins, and I knew Sally-Ann and Jenny were just as excited since they hadn't stopped asking me when they would be meeting Shanelle. Dad and Uncle Mario were the next to arrive. Surprisingly, my father didn't seem very nervous considering that this would be the first time he would be meeting Sally-Ann and Jenny. Shortly after they appeared, Aunt Tina showed up with her husband Joseph, their eldest son Jason and his girlfriend. I was a little confused since I didn't even think her husband, let alone her two sons, had known about my sisters, but I guess they had. It made me think of my Italian grandparents; it was a shame that they couldn't be here simply because of Dad's unwillingness to tell them about the two daughters he had once given away for adoption. It would have been a great opportunity for them to meet Trish and their great granddaughters; who knows when they would have the chance again. It was a good thing that I was too busy to dwell on these thoughts. I thanked God for a beautiful sunny day; it was a little warm on my deck, but at least we could utilize the space.

Everyone was present with the exception of the guests of honor. Trish and Maureen's family finally arrived at 4 p.m., and this time they were late because the kids were enjoying themselves around the hotel pool, and I couldn't blame them. Shanelle came running in from outside, and she hugged Sally-Ann, Jenny and Megan. It was very cute to see their expressions when meeting one another for the first time. The kids ran in the backyard and stopped dead in their tracks when they saw all the people sitting on the deck. Trish came out, hugged everyone, and introduced her daughters to Dad. He hugged them immediately. The girls seemed a bit shy but they returned his hug. My father caught me staring emotionally at him and the girls, and I noticed that he seemed quite emotional himself. I broke that atmosphere by asking him who he thought Jenny resembled, and he laughed as he pointed his finger at me. I could only go by old pictures of myself, and I wanted to know if he remembered what I looked like and if Jenny did, in fact, have similar features or characteristics to me.

Maureen and Trish were introduced to Aunt Tina's family, and they both thought Jason was very good looking. It was too bad that Justin, their other son, couldn't make it. He was equally as handsome. It was nice to see Dad's family support him and want to be part of our family. I spoke to both Aunt Tina and Uncle Mario about their feelings on whether their parents should know about my sisters. They both thought their parents should be told, but that it should come from Dad.

We were all having fun talking, and getting to know my sisters better. When we were taking some photographs, I overheard my father telling Uncle Mario that this day couldn't have happened if it hadn't been for me. I looked over, and they both smiled at me. Once again, I saw that emotional expression on my father's face; he was smiling but I could see his eyes welling up with tears. I couldn't imagine what he was feeling at that moment. I know that I was, personally, still astounded at my new extended family, so he must have been overwhelmed watching his entire family together as it was supposed to be.

I'm sure that even in his wildest dreams, he would never have thought that he would see us all together, interacting so well. I'm sure he thought of his late wife and how regrettable it was that she wasn't by his side, sharing this joyous time. I think he believed, as I did, that she was up in heaven watching us and smiling down on what she had helped happen. I still believed that we wouldn't be here, celebrating our new sisters, had she not passed away.

The day had gone well, and I felt that Dad had gotten a little closer to the rest of his family. However, I did not know how long this would last. I was always a little wary of Dad meeting his daughters. I knew he would be respectful, perhaps a little quiet, but I had witnessed his refusal the first time I had located them, and I didn't want that to happen again. I still had no idea what I expected to happen with Dad. Perhaps I thought that he would, like me, see this as the missing piece from his life, but somehow, he never saw it like that; somehow, something always got in the way - pride, embarrassment, shame, who knows?

On Tuesday morning, Tina, Shanelle and I took Trish's family to Wonderland for the day. Luckily, the weather was beautiful, and we were as pumped up as the kids when we arrived. We purchased our tickets and as we started walking towards the children's area, Trish noticed an awesome roller coaster. She looked like a kid in a candy store, jumping up and down and pulling on my arm, begging me to go on it with her. I was quite apprehensive since it looked a little scary, but I eventually gave in.

Sally-Ann was very brave and wanted to go on all the adult rides, but wasn't able to because of the height restrictions. Shanelle was a little more conservative, but still the two of them went on as many rides as they could. Jenny went on some kiddy rides and she loved them. I couldn't believe the energy this little three year old girl had, and this energy never seemed to cease. At one point, Tina, Trish and I were with Jenny waiting for the others to finish a ride when all of a sudden, we didn't know where Jenny was. We all quickly went searching for her in different directions. My stomach was in my throat as I screamed her name and scurried around the area. She wasn't even my daughter, and I couldn't imagine what Trish was going through at that moment. I couldn't find Jenny, so I went back to where we lost her and to my relief, Trish was holding Jenny's hand. We all felt very guilty for not paying attention. Kevin was not very impressed with us, when Trish told him what had happened, but he understood how it could happen since children, especially children like Jenny, were so fast.

We ate some traditional Wonderland funnel cakes before leaving. We were all extremely tired, but agreed that it had been a fun day together at Wonderland.

On Wednesday, Trish's family came to my house and from there, we visited Gord's father, John. This would be the first time my father-in-law would meet Trish, who he had heard so much about. He had already met Maureen and thought she was a lovely girl, but didn't think she looked at all like me. I introduced Trish, Kevin and the girls to John and his girlfriend, Bernadette. They thought Sally-Ann and

Jenny were the cutest. Trish whispered to me that John was quite the looker, and I laughed and agreed.

We swam, and had fun as we sat and talked around my father-in-law's pool. The girls had a blast in the pool. John thought Trish and I really resembled one another and had the same physique. I noticed that myself when I saw Trish in her leopard print bikini. She had a great figure, and it was hard to believe she had given birth twice. I was training hard at the gym to maintain a good body; however, Trish never worked out or dieted, yet she looked fabulous. Both Tina and Trish were genetically gifted.

John and Bernadette were very gracious hosts. John took a video of us and said that he would give me a copy to send to Trish. He truly is a generous, thoughtful person, and I'm glad his son, my husband, inherited those wonderful traits from him. We discussed our plans for the next day. Trish and Kevin thought it was a good idea to visit Memère Rose since this would be their only opportunity and they wanted her to meet their daughters. I couldn't have been happier with their decision since I knew what it would mean to Memère Rose. We thanked John and left fairly soon as we had to leave early the next morning to get to Memère Rose's house.

It was now Thursday, and we were visiting Memère Rose. The drive to Marmora was two hours and somewhat confusing, so I offered to drive Trish and Kevin's hired station wagon. It was a long journey for the kids, but Sally-Ann and Jenny were great. I noticed how well they played together during the past week, and it was great to see two sisters who loved one another so much. I was really looking forward to this visit, not only because Memère Rose would be meeting her great-granddaughters, but also because it would give Memère Rose and Trish an opportunity to get to know each other better. I just hoped that Memère Rose was feeling okay since she never completely recovered from her heart problems. She didn't have a heart condition after she had the pacemaker, but she lost some of her memory and became easily confused. Leandre was looking forward to meeting them all for the first time since he wasn't present to meet Trish when she last came.

My heart beat faster as we approached their house. Trish and Kevin were astonished at how huge the house was, as well as the size of property they were on. Memère Rose and Leandre were waiting on the front porch for us, and they stood up when they saw our car pulling into the driveway. Surprise, surprise, I was feeling emotional.

The girls jumped out of the car and stood still when they reached the porch. I ran and hugged Memère Rose and Leandre, and introduced the girls to them. Jenny was only three, so when she saw Leandre, she stared at him at first since he was completely bald. Memère Rose hugged them and as with all children, they warmed to her instantly. She thought Jenny resembled Mom more than me, but it was mostly because Mom had curly blonde hair when she was three. Trish gave Memère Rose a hug and introduced herself to Leandre. Kevin shook both their hands and complimented them on their beautiful home.

We all went inside and sat in the family room. The girls went running through the house on their own little tour and came back saying that the house was huge. Trish gave them some paper and crayons to keep them occupied while the adults conversed. Surprisingly, Kevin and Trish didn't have a problem with Leandre's and Memère Rose's French accent; in fact, Kevin spoke in depth with Leandre about different things.

Memère Rose brought out her photo albums as she had with Maureen. Trish was fascinated to see old photos of her birth mother and of us. She came across the picture of Mom as a baby, and as she had done earlier at my house, she again expressed her desire to have a copy of it. Memère Rose promised she would have one made for her and sent to England. We went on the back veranda, and I took photos of us together since I wasn't sure if we were ever going to have this opportunity again. Memère Rose started explaining, yet again, the reasons for having to give Trish away for adoption. Trish tried to ease Memère Rose's mind by telling her that it didn't matter and that she had wonderful parents and held no resentment, but Memère Rose still felt the need to explain.

It hurt me to see Memère Rose not quite herself since her health problem. She repeated herself often about the adoptions, and I knew it was important to her and she felt guilty, but I constantly tried to reassure her that the girls were fine and they didn't blame her. We lived in the present now, and I wanted all of us to be thankful that we still had the rest of our lives to spend together as a family.

It was good to see Memère Rose and Trish talk and laugh together as I had envisioned them doing. When I listened to the two of them, I realized that they actually had very similar personalities. Both women were very strong, independent and motivated individuals. Some people would use the phrase, "they wear the pants in the family," and I found this an enduring quality. There was no doubt in my mind that they would both live a long, rich life. Memère Rose was turning 79 this year and through all her hardships and her recent, near-death experience, she still looked great and was able to talk and laugh. She was becoming very forgetful, and she wasn't able to be very physically active, but she didn't complain. It was just so wonderful that she was alive and well to meet her two great-granddaughters.

Sally-Ann and Jenny colored a picture for Memère Rose and Leandre, and Memère Rose hung it on her refrigerator. She hugged them, and told them how nice and beautiful they were. Eventually, Jenny warmed to Leandre, and he joked and played with the girls. Leandre loved children, and it was unfortunate that he never had any of his own, but he considered himself lucky that we had lived with him and Memère Rose for ten years. He certainly had his fair share of kids laughing, crying, and fighting.

I knew Memère Rose wasn't feeling the greatest, so we gracefully declined dinner and thanked her for her invitation. We said our goodbyes, and the girls told Memère Rose that they wished they could stay longer, which made Memère Rose's face just beam with joy. It was great seeing how happy Memère Rose and Leandre were after meeting the girls. Kevin and Trish were thrilled that they had time to talk and get to know Memère Rose and Leandre better.

We drove home with full bellies after dining at a local restaurant. The girls slept most of the way. Trish thanked me for taking them out to visit Memère Rose, and I just wanted to get home from a long, but very rewarding day. Tomorrow, we were heading for the cottage, and we were all looking forward to being together again.

It was Friday morning, and I was pumped about the cottage. My only concern was that our entire family was coming up for the weekend, and the lady I rented the cottage from seemed adamant that there could only be a maximum of eight overnight guests at one time. I shared my concerns with Tina, Lenny, Rocky and Maureen, but they all instructed me to relax and said that the lady wouldn't even find out. I was ignorant regarding cottage life, so I felt comfortable with their lack of concern since they all had quite a bit of exposure to a cottage. We decided that the rest of the family should arrive after Trish and I had met with the owners to give them their deposit. I told the owner that we would arrive at around 1 p.m., and I certainly didn't want her to see all the extra people.

I felt bad for leaving Gord at home, but he was extremely busy at work. He said he'd be fine - besides, he never liked staying overnight away from home - and he would drive up on Sunday to visit and have dinner with us. I waited for Trish's family to arrive at my house since they were going to follow me in their car. I had to bring my own car since I needed to come back home for a couple of days to work. There was also no way that the stuff I had in my car for the cottage could have been taken in just their vehicle. When they arrived, we said our goodbyes to Gord and we were off. I had to drive alone in my car since it was fully loaded; I had everything from lounge chairs and blankets to food. I wanted this week to be perfect.

As I was driving in front of them, I couldn't help but think of my new family and my past childhood. It still felt unreal to have two more sisters and several more nieces. The family I was raised in was so different from what it was today. I didn't have a mother now, but I had two wonderful sisters and their families. I felt so blessed at this point in my life.

I felt as if I was a child again, reliving the past that I had been denied with my sisters and our entire family. Perhaps others felt differently. Perhaps to them, these were just meetings; times spent with family, times spent with new people. But to me, it was a way of grasping something that had been irretrievably lost; something that couldn't come around again. I was determined to make the most of every moment with my sisters; I wanted to remember each and every second.

We stopped off for lunch at a well-known fast food establishment called Weber's. It was such a busy place that they had built a bridge across the highway so that commuters could stop in both directions and walk safely across. The line-up was as long as usual, but we were too starving to care. After thoroughly enjoying their famous hamburger and fries, I noticed what time it was and realized we were definitely going to be late. I grew concerned that the rest of the gang would arrive while the owners were still there.

The owners were waiting for us when we arrived. I apologized for our tardiness. They didn't appear to be upset, and the lady walked me around the cottage and explained everything I'd need to know. The hot tub upstairs was out of order, but apparently a repairman would be coming in a day or so to fix it. I noticed post-it notes everywhere with rules written on them, so I became very aware that I was dealing with a perfectionist, and this was in fact their full time residence. I wasn't impressed by all these rules, but I gave her the money. I just wanted them to leave before the others arrived. Unfortunately, a car pulled up at the driveway with Lenny, Rocky and Pip followed soon by another car, carrying Tina, Shanelle, Maureen and Megan.

I began panicking as the owner asked them all questions about the duration of their stay. Trish and Kevin were telling me not to worry as I panicked, but I was just caught in a lie and felt totally embarrassed. The owners finally left and as everyone unpacked and settled in, the phone rang. The owner said she was disappointed that I had lied to her and that there would be a $50 per person surcharge for each night. Her calculations came to an extra charge of $350. I told her that I wasn't expecting them all to stay the same night. She didn't budge on the amount, but I didn't argue with her. After hanging up the phone, I told my family about it and they were fine with paying the extra money. I started drinking immediately to calm down, and the phone rang twice more, but I didn't answer. The owner was obviously a little obsessive, and she was making me nervous about the possibility of hidden cameras around the house.

I did not want anything to spoil the weekend, but I could already feel it slipping away from me. However, I did what I could to forget about the owners and my caught red-handed lie, as we made dinner and began our weekend of fun together. The kids finally drifted to sleep at 10:30 p.m. and now, the fun really began. In our drunken stupor, Lenny suggested we play a game that tested our flexibility. There was a beer box on the ground, and the object of the game was to pick it up with your teeth by bending down from a standing position, but you weren't allowed to use your arms. Rocky looked like an ostrich bobbing for his prey, and we couldn't stop laughing. The box kept getting shorter since Lenny would tear off an inch each time. The game finally came down to Kevin and me. I warned him to stop since I was quite fit and somewhat agile, and I knew he was hyper extending. The alcohol was making him think he could force his body into positions that they shouldn't be in. I came out the winner, and Kevin said I was lucky. It was awesome having this much fun with my sisters and brothers and their other halves.

We spent the night laughing and playing like children; every time something remotely funny happened, we would hoot with laughter until our mouths ached. I remember thinking this is what it might have been like all those years ago if our lives had been different.

We had to awake early the next morning because I had booked us all on a boat cruise around Muskoka. With Lenny and Pip leaving later that day, I thought it was a good idea to do some sort of family outing. But now, I was slightly regretting it not only because of our hangovers, but because it was raining heavily. We made the most of our time on the steamboat, and Kevin and Trish thought Lake Muskoka was beautiful. Kevin's hip and lower back were aching as I suspected they would be from our little game. I didn't say, "I told you so," but I did have a little chuckle.

The weather cleared just in time for a barbeque dinner, and we all took part in the preparation and cleaning up. I was missing Gord, but he called and said he'd be coming the next day and would stay for dinner. Lenny and Pip left shortly after dinner, and their absence was definitely felt; they were certainly the life of the party, wherever they went.

I awoke on Sunday morning with a smile on my face; it was wonderful to be spending so much time with my family, even if it seemed to be raining non-stop. I lay in bed thinking it must be quite early since I couldn't hear the children. I stayed in bed enjoying the solitude and feeling fortunate for what I had in my life; a wonderful husband, a part time job that had allowed me the spare time required for my family in the last couple of years, and most of all, a close-knit family. Maureen and Trish were wonderful additions to my family and strangely enough, I started referring to my family before they were part of it, as my "original family." We all seemed closer after meeting our sisters and that was probably due to seeing one another more often.

Gord arrived at noon, and I ran and gave him a big hug. All our nieces ran to him and hugged him. It was another rainy day, and we were joking with Trish and Kevin that they had brought their English weather with them. It was really unfortunate for the kids since they wanted to play outside and go in the lake, but instead had to amuse themselves in the cottage. It was Jenny's third birthday, and we had a little birthday party for her in the afternoon. We bought her a cake - we asked her to make a wish before blowing out the candles - and had some presents for her to open.

Thankfully, the weather cleared in time for dinner. Gord had brought us great steaks to cook. Dinner was a huge success but went by far too quickly. I didn't want Gord to leave, but he had to be at work early the next morning. I had to leave in a couple of days to work myself, but I was returning on Thursday, for Trish's last night at the cottage before heading back to the airport on Friday evening. I said goodbye to Gord and went back to the various card games that we had been playing during the day.

The next morning was Monday, and it was the day Tina and Rocky would be leaving. Shanelle was staying with Trish's family during their entire stay, and I was driving her home on Friday after seeing off Trish's family at the airport. It was raining again, and I could feel the tension in the air; we were all getting really frustrated with the weather. The phone rang, and it was the owner asking us to stay around until the serviceman came to fix the hot tub, and that put me in a worse mood. I couldn't believe that she was expecting us to be inconvenienced after the way she had treated me about the extra people. However, we did want the tub fixed for the kids as it would give them something to do indoors. I shared my annoyance about the hot tub situation with the owner as I wanted her to know that she was inconveniencing us. The serviceman came at noon and the kids were in it having fun by 2:30 p.m.

I left the next morning with Maureen and Megan. I felt guilty, but had no choice since I had to work. I was confident that Kevin would be fine driving; hopefully he wouldn't get lost without me. Admittedly, I was looking forward to seeing Gord and spending the next two nights in the comfort of my own bed. Maureen and Megan said their goodbyes to Trish's family, and they appeared somber since they had no idea when they'd see each other again.

On our drive home, Maureen and I chatted non-stop while Megan slept. We spoke about our time together with Trish, and the differences in all of our personalities. She agreed with me that we were very different siblings who all had a special uniqueness that complimented one another. I felt that Trish and I were most similar, but Maureen didn't agree. She still thought that Tina and I had the most similarities, not only physically, but in our characteristics as well. Considering that we grew up together for seventeen years, I would have thought we would pick up some of the same mannerisms. I thought that my voice and expressions were very much like Tina's. Trish and I, on the other hand, had the same laugh; we both inhaled as we laughed, as if mimicking a bird.

I worked at the office on Wednesday and caught up on all the correspondence. I gave Trish a quick call at the cottage to ensure everything was fine. I was also wondering if the psycho landlady had called to harass us. Trish sounded happy and asked when I would be driving back as she missed me. I thought it was so sweet of her to say so. I told her that I would leave early the next morning and to expect me by lunchtime.

It was Thursday morning and I woke up early to say bye to Gord before he left for work. I had to get an early start on the road. I almost flew to the cottage since there wasn't any traffic and the weather was surprisingly good. I kept my fingers crossed that it would stay sunny all day so Trish's family could experience at least one day at the cottage that would be more typical of our summer. When I arrived, the girls came running to give me a hug, and it felt great being an aunt, or "Auntie," as they called me.

Us girls decided to go for lunch and then, to a candle making store. Kevin stayed behind since he wasn't feeling well, and besides, he wasn't really interested in shopping. We had fun making our candles and brought them home to show Kevin.

That evening, we sat and talked about the time we had spent together; it felt good to be a part of this extended family. We were a whole unit now and whatever happened, we would have each other.

The next morning, we quickly ate breakfast as Trish and Kevin made their final preparations to leave. I felt as if I was losing a part of me. Even though it had only been a few days, I had become so used to seeing my big sister, and I was sad that it was coming to an end.

Shanelle came with me in my car and Kevin followed us. Shanelle said she had a great couple of weeks with her cousins and wished they lived here. I smiled, put my hand on Shanelle's hand, and said, "I wish they lived here too." We stopped off for lunch before we went to a mall, close to the airport, that had a mini amusement park inside. It was a little expensive, but the three girls had a blast.

It was then the dreaded time to drive to the airport. They had to drop the car off, and I told them that Shanelle and I would meet them at their airline counter. We waited for over twenty minutes before I realized we were at the wrong counter, and we ran to the correct one where they were waiting for us as they had already checked in. They wanted to wait outside the gate with Shanelle and I for as long as possible. We sat and ate once again in the terminal, and as Trish was thanking me for everything I started crying. Then Trish got all teary eyed which set Shanelle off. We were all a blubbering mess, and Kevin just shook his head. He couldn't speak since his throat was sore, and I felt bad for him for having to travel in the condition he was in. For one last time, Shanelle and I hugged everyone as tears rolled down our cheeks, before we ran back to my car. At one point, we actually started laughing at ourselves for being so emotional.

After dropping Shanelle off at home, I took a deep breath and sighed. The two weeks were over. I needed to rest and decide what to do with my life.

SISTERS REVEALED

14.
LIFE JOURNEYS

Suddenly, Gord and I were alone together. I had spent all these years searching for my sisters, and now that they had been found, I began to examine how things were in my own life, and what was important.

I made my final attempt at getting pregnant in late January of 2002, and I wouldn't receive the results until early February. I felt really lonely; I suspected it was because I missed Trish and her family. The month of January was usually a little depressing for me due to the cold, freezing weather and the post holiday blues. However, this time it seemed worse. The pressure I had inflicted on myself with the pregnancy attempt may have caused it because, in my mind, I decided that this would be the absolute, final try. We had to stop the disappointment at some stage and get the fun back into our marriage.

I didn't even try to guess if I was pregnant this time, since the progesterone prescribed by the doctor gave me symptoms of being pregnant. It was Monday morning when I had my pregnancy test. I was over the first twelve days again, so I felt a little more optimistic. Gord was at home with me, waiting for the call back. He knew that I would need his support this time, especially since this was my final attempt. If it was negative, I would be crushed.

The phone rang and I jumped to get it. Beth, once again, informed me that it was negative. I told her that she would probably never see me again. I hung up the phone and asked Gord to leave because I wanted to be alone. He hugged me, and respected my wishes and left the house. I didn't want him to witness my pain, but more than that, I didn't want to see his. I didn't have to look into his eyes to sense his great disappointment. What I wanted more than anything was to give him a child after all these years together, and I was unsuccessful in all my attempts. I lay on the couch and cried like a baby. Once again, filled with self-pity, I screamed aloud, "That's it! That was my last attempt." I knew that the never-ending disappointment of failing to get pregnant was starting to take a toll on our marriage and I couldn't let that happen.

Gord came home and he looked exhausted. I sat him down and told him that I wouldn't be trying again, and that we just had to get on with our lives and not look back. Besides, we had given it our best shot, and now I didn't feel guilty or selfish for not having a child. I felt that Gord was more frustrated than usual since he couldn't change the outcome in this instance. However, he was relieved with what appeared to be my coming to terms with never having a child of my own. I wanted to become busier at work or have a career change altogether. Gord didn't want to lose me at our company but he agreed that a part time career would probably be a good thing for me.

In some ways I felt free of the pressure of trying to conceive. I felt relieved of the burden of trying; hope can hurt too, sometimes.

The situation, however, was made worse by the fact that soon after I had come to this decision, Tina fell pregnant. She mentioned being at the doctor's, and I asked her what was wrong. Tina became quiet. The silence scared me, but when I began accusing her of hiding something really bad, she started giggling and said that she was fine. That's when it dawned on me that she might be pregnant. I didn't really believe it, but I asked her anyway. Tina responded by telling me that the pregnancy was unexpected. She told me how excited Steve was and how she wanted a sibling for Shanelle. I asked her if Shanelle knew about the pregnancy, and she said that I was the first person to find out. Tina explained how she had just gone off the birth control pill and had unexpectedly conceived the following month. Needless to say, I was shocked, but I wanted to see her happy. I was thrilled for her as long as she wanted this as much as Steve. I asked her if she was happy since there wasn't a lot of excitement in her tone of voice. Tina said that she and Steve were very happy and couldn't wait to tell Shanelle and Steve's daughter, Sydney. I think Tina was a little nervous to tell me because of my failed attempts at getting pregnant and if she was, then she knew me well.

I cried hysterically after speaking with Tina. It had nothing to do with Tina being pregnant but everything to do with me not being able to conceive. I was happy for Tina and sad for myself. Gord and I had so much love to give a child, and now Tina was having the child I so desperately wanted for us. Tina did mention throughout our conversation how difficult it was going to be for her to tell her sister-in-law Pam since she and her husband had tried to get pregnant for years and, like Gord and myself, were still childless. I actually felt sorry for Tina since this should have been a really happy announcement for her. She shouldn't have felt guilty about telling Pam and I, although I'd have felt the same way if I were in Tina's shoes.

My heart felt like it had been ripped out. This was not because of someone purposely hurting me, but because both my best friend and sister were pregnant - in fact, they were due within a month of each other - and here I was, trying to get over the decision to never again attempt to get pregnant. I managed to pull myself together enough to call Gord and tell him Tina's news but as soon as he answered, I couldn't speak and just cried. He was, naturally, very concerned and told me to calm down and take a deep breath. I finally blurted out that Tina was pregnant and he went quiet. I knew he felt my pain, but instead of saying anything negative, he told me to think on the bright side; I was going to have another niece or nephew and, if they were anything like Shanelle, they would bring so much joy to my life. I knew all that, but my overwhelming self-pity got the better of me. He told me he loved me and would be home as soon as he could. I actually didn't want him home right away since I wanted to be alone with my feelings.

The summer of 2002 went by surprisingly quickly for me. I decided to get a personal trainer's certification for myself and for possibly working part-time at the gym. I was inspired after seeing a friend of mine, Dean, come first place at a natural bodybuilding competition in July. We became quite close friends, not because we lived similar lives, but because we connected emotionally. The gym was a big part of my life, and it not only kept me fit but allowed me to release some of my negative energy. I studied hard for the trainer's exam and passed it in late August. Gord was proud of me, and I was actually proud of myself as well, because I had finally accomplished something on my own - and it felt great.

I didn't notice that Gord and I had drifted apart until the summer was almost over. I did not know whether I had been too busy with other things; too busy with my sisters or with myself, to realize that Gord and I were becoming strangers. Somehow, along the way, we had become two people again instead of a couple. I looked around at my life and did not recognize who I was before all this had begun. I was growing stronger as a person but it meant I was losing Gord. I no longer needed someone to lean on quite so much; the contact with my sisters had changed me, changed the course of my life, and I was unsure whether I was the same person as I once was.

    I started seeing a therapist in order to put some perspective on things, and for a while it helped. During one of my earlier sessions, I discussed my family with her; in particular, the meeting of my two sisters who were given away for adoption. She was happy for all of us and thought a third party was most definitely involved in our finding one another; that third party being Mom's spirit. I told her how positive my relationships with my sisters were, and she was pretty amazed at how well we maintained our friendships. I mentioned Dad's parents not knowing, and how I agonized over whether or not I should be the one to tell them since both my sisters expressed an interest in meeting them. My therapist's initial opinion on the subject was that they probably already knew, but I assured her that they didn't. She then said that she felt it was up to Trish and Maureen to find them and tell their grandparents themselves if that was what they wanted. She felt I should support them, but because I had already had enough involvement in finding them, it was time to step back and not jeopardize my great relationship with my grandparents. I listened to her advice, but naturally, I would do what my heart told me to do.

    On the drive home, I thought about what my therapist said, and I realized that she had some valid points. I was close to my grandparents, and I didn't want anything to interfere with our relationship. I didn't exactly feel that Trish and Maureen should knock on their door and say, "Guess what, we're your granddaughters," but I did think that it would be best to inform Dad about their intentions. This way, Dad would be given time to tell his parents himself, to avoid what could potentially be a heart wrenching moment for them, which considering their age, could possibly affect their health. However, I truly believed that after the initial shock, they would be thankful that they had the opportunity of meeting their eldest son's two first born children.

    I knew that my grandmother would most certainly cry when she laid eyes on Maureen since she would probably feel my Mom's presence like the rest of us did. She loved my mother so dearly, and Maureen had a way of bringing her back to us in her smile, her laugh and her appearance. Trish would remind them of their own children since she was very much like our Italian side of the family. However, even with my strong desire for them to meet, I decided I would tell

Trish and Maureen that I couldn't be the one to reveal Dad's secret, but that I would support them in their decision to tell Dad's parents.

During the next week, I spoke to both Trish and Maureen and informed them of my decision. They were a little disappointed, not with me, but with Dad. Trish didn't seem as concerned as Maureen since she wouldn't be in Canada for awhile, but she was still disappointed with Dad. Trish felt that he was being very immature and that he had his chance last summer, when her family was in Canada. She said that she would probably write Dad a letter, advising him of her intention to meet her grandparents one day. I told her that I thought it was a tremendous idea. Maureen seemed more disappointed, and I'm sure it was partly due to the fact that she lived close by and could bump into them at any time. In addition, Maureen was excluded from family functions attended by our grandparents, so I could understand her frustrations. I advised her to discuss her thoughts with Dad.

It felt so important for our grandparents to be told of my sisters. I did not want them to be a secret anymore; I wanted everyone to know them and love them as I did. Things may change; people may change or move away or lose touch, but we owed it to Mom to celebrate the lives she had made and not hide them away. I felt as if it was up to us to give my sisters the love Mom never had the chance to, and part of that was sharing them with my grandparents.

As I thought about my grandparents, I was reminded of a present I had bought them the Christmas before I had met Maureen and Trish. It was a figurine, depicting an angel holding two babies; one in each arm. As I thought about it, the figurine became larger in my mind. I could picture each curve of the dress, each fold in the fabric that wrapped around the angel's legs. I could picture the tiny hands and feet of the babies she held in her arms and I saw the smile upon her face, loving and motherly. My grandparents kept it on the mantelpiece of their living room and they treasured it. Whenever anyone visited, my grandmother would point it out proudly and say her granddaughter, Debbie, had bought it for her.

It was difficult to see that figurine without seeing the image of Mom, and the daughters she never knew. The face of the angel was her face; the arms, her arms. I knew that whatever happened with my grandparents, or Gord and I, or Trish and Maureen, her arms would always be there; ready to hold us, to comfort us, and to catch us if we fell. The angel on the mantelpiece watched over my grandmother, but I knew that the real angel watched over all of us.

EPILOGUE

It is now almost eight years since I first opened the letter from the Catholic Children's Aid Society, giving me the non-identifying information on the two siblings that I didn't even know I had. That information seems a world away from the two people I have met and grown to love since. It seems strange to think how, at the time, it meant so much. The journey that letter took me on has been a long one, but one that has brought all of my family together.

One of the first things I'm asked when I relate my story is, "Why did your mother do it? What makes a young woman in a reasonably stable relationship give away not one, but two children?" This has always been a difficult question for me to answer, and one that will obviously never be fully addressed. It is too simple, I think, to blame any one person or situation; people act in accordance with the beliefs and norms of the time and, as these change, their actions come to appear alien or mystifying. The decision my mother and her mother took was theirs to make, and it seems futile to question or judge them now.

Of course, it is also the case that perhaps if the decision to adopt out had not been made, none of my other siblings, or even I, would have been born at all. Families tend to have a maximum size and the keeping of my two eldest sisters could have meant two less siblings, further down the line. My experiences over the last eight or nine years have taught me one thing at least; that things work themselves out, one way or another.

I still have no idea what prompted me initially to look for my siblings. There was very little waiting involved even though, at the time, it seemed interminable. I have heard stories of families waiting for decades for their siblings, their children or their parents to contact them. Within a year of beginning my search, I had two new sisters, which is not only a testimony to the part that fate played in this story, but also to the diligence and hard work of those agencies who conduct these services. These agencies are under funded and over worked, but their service is so vital, so important in a very real sense to people's lives.

Like many agencies, the CCAS does not look for people; it waits until a person volunteers their information. This can mean that, too often, whole lives pass by without being reunited. I think this makes my story doubly miraculous. However, I have been assured that miracles happen every day in this field, and that it is only those who do not try, who are sure to be disappointed.

The next question people ask, naturally, is what was it like to meet your sisters after so long? This one I can answer. It was like being a child again, all the time we lost, all the Christmases, all the birthdays, all the anniversaries, all suddenly needed to be lived again. I never laugh as much as when I am with my two sisters because we have grown close and become so much a part of each other's lives. The addition of two whole families to ours meant that we began to notice each other more. We did things we would not have ordinarily done. We talked about things that we would not have before. We shared things, feelings, wishes, and sadness that would have been kept to ourselves or passed over before. We were brought together by the love we shared for our mother.

One year, on one of my all too infrequent visits to Trish in England, we decided to go to Paris. It is a short hop over to France from England, and I thought I would never have the chance again. I remember this time with great fondness; it seemed to sum up the new spirit that had been injected into my family by the new additions.

For a time, Trish and I were children in Paris together; we visited restaurants and cathedrals, shopping arcades and bars and we felt free as birds. We were able to do whatever we wanted without any watchful eyes on us; we felt we had been let loose in the city and we loved every minute of it.

In Notre Dame Cathedral, we both lit candles for our mothers. As I lit my candle, I felt a tear roll down my cheek. I silently spoke to Mom and said that I missed her terribly. I felt she could see how happy Trish and I were, together. I also silently said hello to Trish's mother and I hoped she and Mom were pleased with our sisterly relationship. It was strange, but I could almost feel their presence with us. It was almost as if their spirits were right beside us, and the four of us were touring the Cathedral together. I have never told Trish what I was feeling that day since she'd most likely think I was losing my mind. However, I did bask in the joyous serenity I was experiencing.

I noticed Trish seemed quite emotional after lighting the candle for her mother and it was obvious she really missed her. I truly admire Trish's love for this wonderful woman who adopted her and gave her the love she deserved. Maureen did mention on numerous occasions how much she would have liked to have met Mom. I wished they had both had the opportunity of meeting their wonderful birth mother, but we couldn't change history.

Trish and I hold similar opinions; that had the events of our lives not occurred in the manner they did, then we probably wouldn't have the great sister relationship we have today. The passing of our mothers had an enormous impact on our decision to search for each other. In my case, I don't think I would ever have found out that my sisters were given away for adoption had Mom not passed away. When Trish and I spoke about this fact, she agreed somewhat, but said a private investigator would most likely have tracked down Memère Rose, based on her maiden name. I was just so thankful that we found each other in the way we did; us both having the desire to meet.

Both Trish and Maureen had a sense of fate about our meeting and even though there was a sizable amount of human intervention, in the forms of our husbands for example, we were all aware of the many coincidences that happened along the way.

Paris was a watershed moment for me, not just because of my new sister but because it made me see my relationship with my husband in a clear and unfettered way. The one thing that many people who have gone through similar experiences as me will say, is that it affects all of those around you. It is impossible, I think, for it not to, and I am sure that it contributed to my lack of awareness regarding my marital issues.

Although various members of my family were hesitant about what I had decided to do, there was never a doubt in my mind that what I was doing was the right thing. I thought it was what Mom would have wanted, and what her memory deserved, but there were members of my family who thought it best to "let sleeping dogs lie." Their chief concern, I think, was that it would open old wounds that had been left untouched for decades.

My experiences have shown me, however, that the best thing for such wounds is the open air. I didn't want to just find my sisters; I wanted to be proud of them, to show them off, to tell the world that they were part of my family, and to tell them that I loved them as much as Mom would have. It took a great deal of tact and diplomacy to surmount these problems, but again, I think it was worth the effort. Eventually, most of those members of my family who disagreed with my search were won over; even Dad.

I do not suggest that things were easy for my father. As I read over the early passages of this book, I get a very real sense of how fragile my parents were at the time; somehow the teenagers of forty years ago seem younger than those of today. I suppose the media and the various help-groups buoy up our children, and make them grow old before their time. In the 1950s and 60s, teenagers were just beginning to be recognized as a social entity, yet they were still children then. I cannot imagine that a similar situation would happen today; the social mores and attitudes have changed so much.

Whatever their reasons were for doing what they did, I am sure that my parents never lost their love for their daughters. I often felt Mom's hand on my shoulder when I was unsure or nervous. I sometimes thought I felt her guiding me when I did not know where to turn; I always felt as though she was watching over me.

In the first week of June, 2005, my family and I organized a small get together in Florida. By this time, my marriage was getting back on track, and I was considering a new career. Somehow, things were falling into place again. I still hadn't made another attempt at becoming pregnant, as I had resigned myself to the fact that it was not to be. I was just happy to spoil the expanding army of nieces and nephews that I had been blessed with in the last few years.

It felt great to have the family in one place; the faces so startlingly different and yet surprisingly the same. Both Maureen and Trish attended, and again we all felt like children; laughing and joking, getting merry and playing around. At one point during our visit, I sat back and watched all of the smiling faces. It felt dreamlike to be in Florida with the two girls my parents gave away for adoption so many years ago. Everyone accepted and loved them as my sisters, and I knew this would have pleased Mom. I'm sure it also meant a great deal to Dad, although he never really expressed it.

The next couple of days were spent at amusement parks, and what long days they were. I enjoyed the Tower of Terror ride at MGM Studios, but rides and crowds were not really my thing. Trish enjoyed them as much as the kids did. The weather didn't cooperate and it rained almost non-stop. We spent a day together at Uncle Tony's house; it was one of the best times we've had, all of us together as a family.

EPILOGUE

As we sat around the table together at Uncle Tony's, I let my eyes drift over my family. We were one now; a unit that played together, laughed together, and was there together when we needed each other. There was something unsaid between us that was, perhaps, stronger than in most families. The death of Mom had lit a spark that was being kept alive in each of us, and as I looked around the table, I could see it positively glowing.

I always felt sad going home after family trips and holidays, but the trip home from Florida was something different. Somehow, I did not feel sad anymore; I only felt a sense of satisfaction, as if I had completed something or had come to the end of a chapter. I sat on the plane, looked out of the window, and wondered how many people had gone through a similar thing yet had not been so lucky. How many people waited for the phone call that never came? The list was probably endless. I was one of the lucky ones.

When I landed, the terminal was busy; people were rushing here and there, meeting loved ones and leaving friends. There was an air of impatience and annoyance through which I seemed to just drift. I met Gord and we drove home, but I was too tired to really talk. All I wanted to do was retain the memory of the trip for one more hour, perhaps one more day, and then move on with the rest of my life.

I began this book originally as a journal. Perhaps I felt as though I needed to put events in order and to try to make sense of things and perhaps, get some kind of control over them. In writing and researching this book, I had to ask my family, Dad in particular, questions about his and my mother's life that I never thought I would ask. I asked him about how they met - somehow it had never come up in prior conversations - and the story he told (although, I'm sure it was embellished somewhat) was much like any other couple's. My mother, although beautiful all her life, was much like any other Canadian mother of the 1960s and 70s. She would cook our meals, look after us when we were ill, and hold us when we hurt.

Underneath this, however, there was an extraordinary story; a story that begins with the pain of separation but ends with the joy of reunion. There were times, of course, when I thought it was too much for me to trace my sisters; that I could not stand to go through with it anymore. At times, it felt as if I was losing my mind, but somehow, I held on and in the end, that has made all the difference.

I was made aware, as I was writing this book, of all the various stages involved in the process of looking for a lost one or family member, and how best to deal with it. Very few people tell you that every stage has its drawbacks and pleasures. The trials do not simply stop once the person has been found, but continue well after they have been introduced into the family. There are obstacles and hurdles at every turn that may trip the unwary.

At its heart, this book concerns itself with family. Not just in terms of my sisters, Trish and Maureen, but with our wider families and what they mean to us. I gradually became more and more aware of the place of family concerning one's own growth; how they nurture and change us, how they shape our ways of thinking, and how they influence the way we look.

One of the most obvious connections I have with the daughters of my sisters is through the way we look; it is obvious by looking at us that we are of the same blood, and this is more important than we might first think. A physical resemblance is a manifestation of some deeper genetic message - it ensures we are aware of our tribe, of our heritage, and it means that the notion of family is literally inscribed upon our skin. This book is about the extent to which that is true. That even if the physical ties between family members are broken; nature still shines through.

This book is also about hope and determination. It is only through a combination of these two things that I ever managed to reunite with my two sisters at all. Every case of adoption is different; for every person adopted, there is a different tale, a different reason. Some will be more understandable than others. However, what is certain is that my experiences were not unique; they may have been exceptional, but they are not impossible to replicate. I hope my story prompts someone else to begin a similar journey to my own.

Most of all, however, this book is about a mother's love for her children. I am convinced that Mom knew perfectly well what she was doing when she spoke of her lost daughters before she died. She knew that my sisters needed to found and brought into the family that had borne them. She wanted the search to begin at last. Every step of the way I felt her guiding presence, I knew that she was with me and she agreed with what I was doing. She had set me on my way, and I was merely following her path. She didn't do this for herself or Dad or for me; she did it for Trish and Maureen.

Other Voices

Muskoka - Summer 2001

OTHER VOICES

As with all stories, there are other voices, and this is a chance to hear them:

Trish

I grew up a very happy and contented child surrounded by much love from my wonderful parents and a large circle of friends. My parents told me that I was adopted when I was nine years old, an age I consider just old enough to truly understand the full meaning of adoption. I guess in today's world nine seems old as children seem to grow up so quickly these days. My initial reaction was one of numbness. I didn't speak or ask any questions. I just left the room, had a little cry and went out to play.

I never did have any great urge to trace my family. I guess this was a reflection of the contentedness and happiness I had in my life. It was my husband Kevin who persuaded me to search, partly because of my daughter's medical problems but also because he was genuinely interested to know if I had family. My husband comes from a large family himself and is one of five children. He is totally devoted to his family. Thank you Kevin for your persistence!

My expectations weren't high when I initiated the search. I knew the process could be lengthy and I prepared myself for the worst case scenario. I asked my dad if he was ok with me searching and kept him involved throughout the entire process. I also told him how much I loved him and ensured him I wasn't looking for any replacements in my life. My mum had sadly passed away a couple of years previously. I am not sure if I could ever have searched if she was still alive.

I had a vision of my birth mother as a young Catholic girl who had me at a very young age, probably remarried with a family of her own. I never dreamt in a million years of having full blood brothers and sisters, a natural father, and a whole other family. Everything happened so quickly it was hard to take it in. It felt like a rollercoaster ride and my emotions were all over the place. I initiated the search in August 1999 and received that first letter in November by registered post which signaled the start of a whole new life for me.

I was extremely disappointed and upset to learn that my natural mother Nicole had died at such a young age. I can't even begin to imagine what it must have been like for her to give her two babies away. I so wanted to thank her for having me when the alternative could have been to have a termination, and to let her know how blessed I was to have been brought up by two wonderful parents. I wanted her to meet my husband and her two beautiful granddaughters Sally and Jenny.

Once I knew the full extent of my family, I desperately wanted to meet everyone. Kevin & I flew to Toronto on January 28th 2000. What a millennium present this was going to be! The plane journey seemed to take forever. I had seen pictures of everyone so I knew what to expect. My heart was pounding so loudly. As we got off the plane, there they were Tina and Debbie, both as beautiful as the pictures I had seen of them. Once we spoke it was as if we had known each other all our lives and I knew that when the comment was made "she has a bum and boobs" that we would get on like a house on fire.

Over the next couple of days I met my other sister Maureen and my brothers Rocky and Lenny. God, Rocky looks so much like me, it's scary. I met my natural father Rocky senior, an extremely nice and attractive man, aunts and uncles, grandmother, nieces, brother-in-laws, family friends etc. I brought my children to Canada the following summer to meet everyone and to get to know everyone a little better. The distance however makes it difficult.

I consider meeting my family as an added bonus to my life and I know that whilst we never grew up together as a family unit with all the bickering that brothers and sisters have (I was an only child), we have formed a friendship that will continue to grow with time. I owe a huge thanks to my sister and closest friend Debbie for initiating the search to find me. Without you none of this would have been possible. At the same time I haven't lost sight of the two people who brought me up to be the person I am today, and who I owe so much to. Mum and dad, I love you both so very much.

Meeting my brothers and sisters is one of the greatest gifts that life has brought my way and I treasure this with all my heart.

Love you heaps Debs

Trish

Maureen

"Ever since I was a young girl and was told that I had been adopted there has been an emptiness in my life. Many times, thoughts of who my real parents were and where they might be ran through my mind. Not knowing why I had been given up, or where my life might be had circumstances been different, tore at my heart.

As years passed and I started a family of my own, I realized how important it was to live each day to the fullest and be happy for what I had been given.

With the support of family and friends, I decided to register with Children's Aid in the hopes of finding out any information on my birth parents or family. The events that followed within the next few months after the letter was sent would change my life forever. The news of my birth mother passing away saddened my heart, but finding out that my father was still alive and that I had other brothers and sisters made me very happy.

Tears of pain quickly became tears of joy. When I found out that there was another daughter put up for adoption, I didn't feel so alone. Over the years, I have had a chance to meet most of my family members and share many special times together. With each passing year, the emptiness that once consumed my life has been filled with wonderful memories. This has allowed me to find the strength to move on and be a better person.

With all said and done the best way to describe my life as it is now would be, complete."

Tina

"It was 8:30 on a Saturday night in November when the phone rang. This was the call that would change my life forever. What is she like? Does she have curly hair, green or blue eyes? Does she look like Mom or Dad? I couldn't ask the questions fast enough. Much to my surprise, this would be the night I would be meeting one of the two sisters that were kept as a big secret my whole life. A rush of emotions swept over me. I was anxious and scared and I didn't have a thing in the house to offer her. What kind of first impression will that make? I tidied up and rushed to the corner store so that I could least offer coffee or tea. Minutes seemed like hours. Was I ready for this? I heard a car door slam and ran to the window to get a glimpse, but it was much too dark to see. Next thing I knew, she was standing in my doorway.

Any words I was prepared to say were overcome by the lump in my throat and the tears in my eyes. I threw my arms around Maureen and hugged her like a long lost friend; someone I had known my whole life. Once the tears subsided, we talked and talked, trying to get answers to all the questions. I recall saying how much she resembled Mom; her hands and the twinkle in her eyes. I dug out old photos from our childhood with Mom and Dad, and all the rest of us for her to see. That's when she pulled out a photo of her daughter, Megan, and I remembered how delighted I was to find out I was an aunt, something I wondered if I would ever be. After she left, I remember feeling relieved and excited. I couldn't wait to share the news of that evening with my friends.

Almost one year to the day after finding Maureen, I received a call from my sister Debbie. "They've found our other sister and she lives in England!" It was nothing short of a miracle. What were the chances of finding them both, especially with one living thousands of miles away? It made me realize that my mother's death had a purpose. We were all meant to be together. Nothing could replace the loss of a mother but at least we were given two sisters in return.

It was a chilly day in January when I met Trish. I couldn't wait to meet her, to see who she resembled and to hear her British accent. I remember waiting at the airport with Debbie eyeing every woman that came through arrivals, looking for that one girl who could be our sister. A rush of emotion came over me as Trish headed towards us and once again, the tears spilled down my face. We hugged and I immediately felt a connection. She was most definitely one of us, although looking more like one from my father's side of the family. As I did with Maureen, I had so many questions for Trish and wanted to know everything about her. I loved listening to her speak as I am very fond of the British accent, although I do have to say that there were moments where I wasn't quite sure what she was saying. She talked of her girls, Sally Anne and Jenny and I remember how pleased I was to be blessed with two more nieces. We parted that night and once again, I couldn't wait to share the news of our meeting.

Even now, I sit sometimes and wonder what my life would have been like, growing up as one of the middle children and not the oldest. Would I be a different person today? Growing up as the oldest child, I always felt I had to be the responsible one, the obedient one; the daughter who tried to maintain some sort of control and order in the household when my Mom was at work. I struggled between pleasing my mother and living my life as I wanted. Some of the rules she imposed on me seemed selfish and senseless at the time, but I now understand and respect her decisions. It was the only way she knew to prevent history from repeating itself. Would things have been different if we'd had Trish and Maureen in our lives then? I suppose that's something I'll never know.

So, what does it mean to me to have two additional sisters in my life? I guess it's giving me more of what I love most in life - family. Some of my fondest memories are those that were shared with my brothers and sister. Although privacy was unheard of and having a space of my own didn't happen, I wouldn't trade it for the world. I always had someone to share things with, to play with, to laugh with, and to fight with. I was never alone. I think it's wonderful having Trish and Maureen in my life, and I know I've already created some special memories with them and look forward to more in the future."

Lenny

"Despite how devastating it was, the death of my mother has brought some positive aspects into my life such as, inspiring me to further my education and more importantly, strengthening our family bond.

I was quite shocked when I first heard the news about Trish and Maureen. I didn't know how to react - for the first 25 years of my life they were non-existent. It must have been very difficult for my mother to keep this a secret for so long. Were they going to exhibit resentment for my parents giving them up for adoption, or would we be welcomed with open arms?

To my surprise, I didn't feel nervous the first time we met. I wasn't really that excited either, when compared to my other siblings. However, I did feel an obligation to share with them how good Nicole was as a mother when we were growing up. For whatever reason they were given up for adoption, I'm sure it was a good one.

Meeting Trish, Maureen, and their immediate families was quite an experience. The term "big brother" became more relevant to me. It must be comforting to know that they have an immediate blood family they can turn to, particularly for Maureen, who had a disgruntled family upbringing.

Overall, my newfound sisters have only had a little impact on my daily life. For some reason, I communicate very little with either one. I feel privileged to have been brought up with two adorable sisters and a brother who I dearly love; unfortunately, I don't quite share the same sentiments for Trish and Maureen at this time, but I hope that will change in the future.

The coming together of my sisters has deepened my outlook on the importance of maintaining a healthy family circle. It has strengthened the bond we share which has been passed on from our mother and her ancestors.

The effort and perseverance of Debbie in finding our sisters cannot be described in words. I think it is quite remarkable and something my mother would have wanted to pursue in her lifetime – 'Hats off to you, Debbie.'"

Rocky

"It was quite the riveting news I received when answering the phone that afternoon. Debbie was on the line, and I could hear the excitement in her voice. It struck me as strange when she said, "I made contact with our sister." With whom, I asked. "I made contact with our sister," she repeated. She had talked to Tina, I assumed, and I asked if she had some good news. "No, it is the other sister," said Debbie.

What other sister?

Well, whether or not I should have been prepared for that day, I was now one of six siblings; one brother, four sisters (huh!) and me. Heck, we were even global now I had a sister living in England. All of this breaking news probably would have made sense, but it was hard for me to focus when Debbie had told us that there were others. Either it never registered, or I had just been too concerned with Mom's passing.

Many a moment has passed since then and now, and I want to be concise about the effects, and the impressions I have, of my now extended family. Firstly, there are six of us, and we have spawned five more.

When I first met Trish, it was like looking in a mirror - really! We never once questioned whether she belonged; I mean, we could pass as twins. And the oddest thing, is that two people could have six children who all somewhat resemble each other, and yet stunningly, it is the youngest and the oldest who are the spitting image of each other.

Now, Maureen had a different effect on me when we met. I was able to see Mom in her, especially in the way she carried herself, in her hair, and her hands. All wonderful things we missed and were refreshed to see.

Now that seven years have passed (maybe eight or nine) since the extended family revealed itself, I find myself asking, are there any more? What has changed? I must say that it seems like Trish and Maureen have always been a part of us, all along. I visited Trish frequently in England, which was fun and different. This, I have to say, wouldn't have happened if Trish hadn't convinced me to get myself a nice Yorkshire lass. Ultimately, everything has worked out for the best.

Other than birthdays, holidays, special occasions, and regrettably funerals, we as a family do not see each other as often as some. We never did. So do we now attempt to visit more often because of the changes? No. But I keep my family close to my heart; they are very special to me and it's something that is becoming more apparent as we all get older. I wish good health and happiness to them all. No news is good news."

ACKNOWLEDGEMENTS

All opinions, feelings and events are factual based on my memory alone. Family history prior to my birth is my recollection of the memories shared by family members (albeit somewhat embellished). Only my husband has been privy to the contents of the book prior to printing.

Sisters Revealed has gone through several metamorphoses and there are special people to thank.

As a journal I have my family and friends to thank for the life experiences. From a journal I transformed my work into a story with the intent of it being a gift for my family and friends. During the writing process I realized that my story held hope for many people involved in adoption and decided to have it edited for possible publication.

It was at this point that I enlisted the help of Tricia Hills, my dear friend Bryan's daughter to edit my book. Tricia agreed to this challenge during her final year at the University of Guelph as an English major. Seeing that we were both intuitive and spiritual in nature I knew we would make a great team. *I can't thank you enough Tricia for all your hard work and dedication to my project and I wish you a life filled with all good things (remember Libra man).*

Once edited I had Ken, a friend and published author, provide his opinion. This led me to a ghostwriter in the UK named Paul Elliott. Everyone who touched my book up until this point I knew personally however there were two big coincidences with Paul – he lived in the UK like my sister Trish and he shared the same first and last name of a friend of mine (I didn't find out until after I chose him). It was destiny!

Paul, or as I affectionately call you 'Ghost', thank you for helping bring my book to life. From the onset I felt we had a special connection. It was amazing how you were able to assume my persona throughout the entire book and shed new light on my experiences.

How many times did I say to you, "It's as if you were walking in my shoes."

My baby brother Rocky designed the book cover. He works as a graphic artist and excitedly offered to create the cover. How fortunate for me to have someone work with me who walked the same path as I. *Rocky thank you wholeheartedly for extracting my vision and capturing the essence of my book. You're the best!*

A special thank you to Lina at the Catholic Children's Aid Society (CCAS) for helping to bring our families together in a warm and loving way. *Lina, thank you for making that final call to Maureen in an attempt to contact her. Your hope and persistence will not be forgotten.*

An associate of mine, Anita of the Photographic Group of Aurora, Ontario photographed me in my swivel rocker at home for the back cover portrait.

Finally I would like to express my gratitude to my family for trusting me to share intimate and personal portions of their lives. *Your enthusiasm for my book both inspired and provided me with the confidence to publish it. I love each and every one of you.*